PENGUIN BOOKS

MUMMIES

James Hamilton-Paterson has travelled extensively since leaving
Oxford University, where he first acquired his interest in Egyptology.
He has taught in a government secondary school in Libya and been
to Brazil when working for the *New Statesman*. He has also explored
Southeast Asia while researching a book on corruption in the Vietnam
war. More recently, he has lived for a year in Egypt, learning Arabic
and furthering his studies in Egyptology. He is the author of several
books, including three novels, a volume of poetry, and his book on
the war in Vietnam.

Carol Andrews, having read Classics at London University, did a
postgraduate course in Egyptology, after which she joined the department of Egyptian antiquities at the British Museum as a research
assistant. She was closely involved in the hugely successful Tutankhamun exhibition and was responsible for the Egyptian entries in
the museum's exhibition 'Jewellery through 7000 Years'. She is the
author of two British Museum publications: *Private Egyptian Sculpture* and *Ancient Egyptian Jewellery*. While on her visits to Egypt as
a guest lecturer she took many of the photographs that appear in this
book.

MUMMIES

DEATH AND LIFE
IN ANCIENT EGYPT

James Hamilton-Paterson
and Carol Andrews

PENGUIN BOOKS

Penguin Books Ltd, Harmondsworth, Middlesex, England
Penguin Books, 625 Madison Avenue, New York, New York 10022, U.S.A.
Penguin Books Australia Ltd, Ringwood, Victoria, Australia
Penguin Books Canada Limited, 2801 John Street, Markham, Ontario, Canada L3R 1B4
Penguin Books (N.Z.) Ltd, 182–190 Wairau Road, Auckland 10, New Zealand

First published in Great Britain by William Collins Sons & Co. Ltd 1978
First published in the United States of America in simultaneous hardcover
and paperback editions by The Viking Press and Penguin Books 1979

Library of Congress Cataloging in Publication Data
Hamilton-Paterson, James.
Mummies, death and life in ancient Egypt.
Bibliography: p. 216.
Includes index.
1. Mummies.   2.   Funeral rites and ceremonies—Egypt.
3. Tombs—Egypt.   4.   Egypt—Antiquities.
I.   Andrews, Carol, joint author.   II.   Title.
[DT62.M7H35   1979b]   393'.3'0932   79-12901
ISBN 0 14 00.5266 6

Printed in the United States of America by
The Book Press, Brattleboro, Vermont

CONTENTS

DATE	DYNASTY	PERIOD	PHARAOHS	OTHERS
3100 BC	1st Dynasty (3100–2890 BC)	ARCHAIC PERIOD 1st and 2nd Dynasties	Menes	"Ginger"
3000 BC			Djer (c. 3000 BC)	
2900 BC	2nd Dynasty (2890–2686 BC)		Anedjib (c. 2925 BC)	
2800 BC				
2700 BC				
	3rd Dynasty (2686–2613 BC)	OLD KINGDOM 3rd–6th Dynasty	Djoser (c. 2650 BC)	Imhotep
			Huni (c. 2620 BC)	
2600 BC	4th Dynasty (2613–2494 BC)		Sneferu (c. 2600 BC)	Hetepheres
			Khufu (c. 2575 BC)	Djedi
			Khafre (c. 2550 BC)	Ruaben
			Menkaure (c. 2525 BC)	
2500 BC	5th Dynasty (2494–2345 BC)			
				Ti
				Ptahhotep
2400 BC	6th Dynasty (2345–2181 BC)		Wenis (c. 2350 BC)	Waty
2300 BC				
				Khentika Ikhekhi
2200 BC			Pepy II (c. 2200 BC)	
	11th Dynasty (2133–1991 BC)	1ST INTER-MEDIATE PERIOD 7th–11th Dynasty		Ankhtifi
2100 BC			Inyotef (c. 2100 BC)	
			Mentuhotep II (c. 2060–2010 BC)	Gua
2000 BC	12th Dynasty (1991–1786 BC)	MIDDLE KINGDOM 11th–13th Dynasty		Neferti
				Sinuhe
				Ipuwer
1900 BC			Sesostris II (1897–1878 BC)	Hepdjefau
1800 BC				
	13th Dynasty (1786–1633 BC)			
1700 BC				
	15th Dynasty (1674–1567 BC)		THE HYKSOS	
	17th Dynasty (1650–1567 BC)	2ND INTER-MEDIATE PERIOD 14th–17th Dynasty		
1600 BC			Sobkemsaf (c. 1640 BC)	
			Seqenenre II (c. 1580 BC)	
	18th Dynasty (1567–1320 BC)		Ahmose (c. 1570–1546 BC)	
		NEW KINGDOM 18th–21st Dynasty	Amenophis I (c. 1546–1526 BC)	
			Tuthmosis I (1525–c. 1512 BC)	Ineny
1500 BC			Hatshepsut (1503–1482 BC)	
				Paheri
			Tuthmosis III (1504–1450 BC)	Rekhmire
				Amenemhat
			Amenophis II (1450–1425 BC)	Amenemheb
			Tuthmosis IV (1425–1417 BC)	Menna
				Nebamun
			Amenophis III (1417–1379 BC)	Tiye
				Yuya and Thuya

DATE	DYNASTY	PERIOD	PHARAOHS	OTHERS
1400 BC		NEW KINGDOM 18th–21st Dynasty		Amenhotep Son of Hapu Nefertiti
			Akhenaten/Smenkhkare (1379–1361 BC) Tutankhamun (1361–1352 BC)	Huy
	19th Dynasty (1320–1200 BC)		Ay (1352–1348 BC) Horemheb (1348–1320 BC) Ramesses I (1320–1318 BC)	Neferhotep
1300 BC			Seti I (1318–1304 BC) Ramesses II (1304–1237 BC)	Khaemwese
			Merenptah (1236–1223 BC)	Ani Hunefer
1200 BC	20th Dynasty (1200–1085 BC)		Ramesses III (1198–1166 BC) Ramesses IV/VI (1166–1148 BC)	Amenmes Amenemint Anhai
1100 BC			Ramesses IX (1140–1121 BC)	Paser and Paweraa Amenpanefer
	21st Dynasty (1085–945 BC)		Ramesses XI (1113–1085 BC) THE TANITES Psusennes I (1059–1033 BC)	Paikharu
1000 BC			Amenemope (1033–981 BC)	Maatkare Henttawy Isemkheb Nesi-Khonsu
	22nd Dynasty (945–730 BC)			Harnakht
900 BC		LIBYAN PERIOD 22nd–25th Dynasty	Osorkon II (874–850 BC)	
800 BC	25th Dynasty (750–656 BC) 24th Dynasty (730–709 BC)		THE KUSHITES	
700 BC	26th Dynasty (664–525 BC)	LATE PERIOD 26th–30th Dynasty	THE SAITES	
600 BC	27th Dynasty (525–404 BC)			
500 BC				
	28th–29th Dynasties (404–378 BC)			Herodotus
400 BC	30th Dynasty (380–343 BC)			
300 BC		PTOLEMAIC PERIOD 304–30 BC	Alexander The Great (332–323 BC) Ptolemy I Soter (304–282 BC)	
200 BC				
100 BC			Cleopatra VII (51–30 BC)	
Birth of Christ		ROMAN EMPIRE		
100 AD				
200 AD				Artemidorus

INTRODUCTION

If one were to ask almost anybody what first came into their minds at the mention of ancient Egypt, the chances are they would answer 'mummies'. It is ironic that a civilization which flourished so vitally for some three thousand years should now be best known for its dead. Yet the Egyptians themselves, could they have known of their civilization's eventual downfall, would probably not have wished it any other way. For them life after death was of paramount importance. They believed that their spiritual survival depended absolutely on their bodies' physical survival, so they lavished a good deal of ingenuity on the art of preserving dead bodies.

Why did they believe this? Nearing the end of this century, we are conscious of the well-publicized dead of two world wars and unnumbered lesser ones; of the countless million victims of purges, genocide, famine, disaster and disease. We have seen too many pictures of corpses to believe any longer that the survival of our own bodies after death is either likely or important. Many people seek refuge in a belief in some kind of spiritual survival; but as traditional religious faith slowly decays even this belief becomes more shadowy and often amounts to little more than a superstitious hope.

Yet the power of other civilizations' death cults is as strong – if not stronger – than ever. Above all, people still find the ancient Egyptians mysterious and fascinating. It is almost as if we no longer dare show publicly an interest in our own survival, but can still indulge private hopes by studying older cultures whose belief in a life after death was absolute and unquestioned. This may often involve a positively mystical faith that the Ancients actually did have knowledge which is lost to twentieth-century man. All sorts of arcane wisdom – including amazing occult powers – are ascribed by modern wishful thinkers to the ancient Egyptians.

This partly accounts for the unflagging interest in their mummified bodies. In the final chapter of this book we have written about how for centuries Europe imported and used mummy-powder (i.e. ground-up Egyptians) simply out of sheer superstition. Doctors used to prescribe it and artists sometimes mixed it with their colours when painting death scenes. Even nowadays a market still exists for it.

At a popular level ancient Egypt is still surrounded by an aura of considerable mystery. Yet Egyptology has been a subject of intense scholarship for well over a century, and more is known about the Egypt of the pharaohs than almost any other ancient civilization. An enormous quantity of relics has survived besides the mummies and their tombs which includes a massive bulk of written documents, both religious and secular (including literary, legal, medical, military and governmental texts). It is true that there are still things we do not know or cannot understand fully; yet there is surprisingly little of importance which remains a total mystery. This is true even of the Egyptians' religion. If there is plenty which is obscure – for example parts of their magical books and spells – it is often because the Egyptians were themselves none too clear about much of what they believed. A good deal of what we find meaningless and contradictory was meaningless and contradictory when it was laboriously copied down.

The truth is that the Egyptians' religion was an enormous hodge-podge of different theologies, legends, theories, myths and old wives' tales. Which belief was uppermost depended on the time and the place. In Memphis they believed one thing and in Heliopolis another. Unravelling all these beliefs requires an act of scholarship, not one of necromancy.

Our first task, therefore, is to acquire some idea of who the Egyptians were and what they believed in. It would be pointless to describe in gruesome detail *how* the upper-class Egyptians mummified their dead unless something is first known about *why* they did it. Once we have understood what they hoped to achieve, their funerary customs will seem far less absurd or mysterious. They do remain complicated, however, which unfortunately makes the first chapter of this book more difficult than the others.

What people cannot understand they generally ignore or call a mystery. It is evident that the mummies of ancient Egypt continue to prove hard to ignore and that even now, when there are plenty of facts available, there are some people who actually prefer to be mystified. For those who do not, we hope this book will at least help dispose of one or two common misconceptions. We also hope that by the end the reader will have realized that there is little 'mystery' surrounding Egyptology other than that which is wilfully brought to it, apart from the mysteriousness inherent in all matters of mortality and the passage of time.

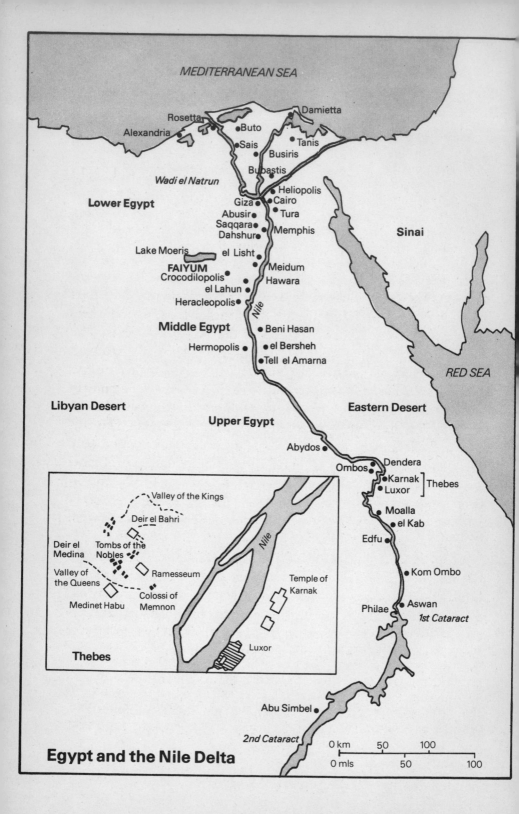

MEDITERRANEAN SEA

Rosetta
Damietta
Alexandria
Buto
Sais
Tanis
Busiris
Bubastis

Wadi el Natrun

Lower Egypt

Heliopolis
Giza
Cairo
Abusir
Tura
Saqqara
Memphis
Dahshur

Sinai

Lake Moeris
el Lisht

FAIYUM
Meidum
Crocodilopolis
Hawara
el Lahun
Heracleopolis

Middle Egypt

Beni Hasan
Hermopolis
el Bersheh
Tell el Amarna

Nile

Libyan Desert

Upper Egypt

Eastern Desert

RED SEA

Abydos

Dendera
Ombos
Karnak ⎤
Luxor ⎦ Thebes

Moalla
el Kab

Edfu

Kom Ombo

Philae
Aswan
1st Cataract

Valley of the Kings

Deir el Bahri

Deir el
Medina
Tombs of the
Nobles

Valley of
the Queens
Ramesseum

Nile

Temple of
Karnak

Medinet Habu
Colossi of
Memnon

Thebes

Luxor

Abu Simbel

2nd Cataract

0 km   50   100

0 mls   50   100

Egypt and the Nile Delta

I

THE BACKGROUND

The Place

Egypt is the Nile. That is to say, the River Nile prevents part of Egypt from becoming just another tract of barren wilderness dotted with dunes, rocks, scrub and the occasional oasis. The White Nile and the Blue Nile spring deep inside Africa and join at Khartoum in the Sudan to flow northwards through Egypt and out at the Delta into the Mediterranean. Regularly each year the distant African rainfall swells the river into a flood which, until the completion of the first Aswan Dam in 1902, would inundate the Nile Valley in Egypt between July and October, the water bringing with it huge quantities of mud and silt. These deposits of mud were extremely fertile and in consequence the Nile Valley, with its endless supply of water and regular fertilization, was a Garden of Eden compared with the desert on either side.

From archaeological evidence it seems there have always been settlers in this valley – at least since Paleolithic times. Gradually these people gathered in certain areas and formed different cultures so that it is possible to make generalizations about them which distinguish between the cultures of Upper Egypt to the south and Lower Egypt in the north.

The History

For the purposes of this book we shall take Egyptian history as beginning roughly at the time when a written language first appeared and Upper and Lower Egypt had become united into a single administrative entity. This point marks the beginning of the period known as Dynastic which lasted about three thousand years, from some four hundred years before the building of the first pyramid almost until the time of Christ. This encompasses what is popularly thought of as 'ancient Egyptian civilization'. The term 'dynastic' comes from the work of a historian-priest named Manetho who was the first known person to compile a complete list of all the pharaohs of Egypt. He divided nearly three thousand years of continuous history into thirty dynasties which later historians have further grouped into the Old Kingdom, the Middle Kingdom, the New Kingdom and the Late Period. Between the Old and the Middle and the Middle and the New come two short gaps when for various reasons the country became ungovernable as a whole and the succession of pharaohs broke down into a rabble of lesser rulers. These gaps are known respectively as the 1st and 2nd Intermediate Periods. At the very end of the Late Period, after the 30th Dynasty, Egypt was ruled by kings of Greek descent. This is known as the Ptolemaic Period and was followed by the Roman Period when Egypt was occupied as part of the Roman Empire. Schematized, Egyptian dynastic history looks like the table shown on the endpapers.

The People

By the time of the Old Kingdom the Egyptians' was a flourishing civilization with well-developed literary, artistic and scientific abilities. It also had a highly sophisticated governmental and legal system based on careful codification and libraries of written records. Nothing could have been further removed from the tribesmen who roamed Europe at this time, dressed in skins, living in caves and with weapons no more sophisticated than flint axes. In its bureaucratic and legal aspects ancient Egypt was much like any modern state run by civil servants in accordance with the law of the land. Its body of statutes and precedents was carved, inscribed, painted and memorized, and these laws both reflected and bolstered the central strength of Egypt's philosophy: a belief in the importance of change-lessness.

The countryside of Egypt was peculiarly suitable for the growth of such a philosophy. The climate was more or less uniform and there were no cataclysms like volcanoes – and only the occasional earth tremor – to contend with. There was too much inhospitable desert to be crossed to make the country irresistibly attractive to invaders on either side. Life flowed on undisturbed like the Nile in its immemorial bed. The seasons came round with strict punctuality, the Nile flooded, crops sprang up. It is small wonder that, unaffected by outside contacts and with an orderly and stable society apparently as old as creation itself, the Egyptians believed that the world was static. If there were ever any changes to be seen, they were of a recurrent variety: the cyclical changes of nature. Any other events were nothings, momentary ripples on the surface of the great stream of eternity which soon effaced themselves and were lost. As a result the Egyptians, being almost entirely an agricultural people, closely identified themselves with the natural world; and out of this identification sprang a characteristic aspect of their religious beliefs.

Animal Cults

For the Egyptians the animal world possessed a peculiar, and to us elusive, significance. They worshipped an enormous variety of animals from millipedes to bulls, some of which were only sacred locally while others were sacred throughout Egypt. It is tempting to try and make sense of this phenomenon by proposing such theories as 1) the animals each had a different characteristic which made them worthy to be worshipped, or 2) animals peculiar to a particular locality were used for political reasons to hold a tribe together around a common god.

Unfortunately, such theories never quite meet all the facts and are true only some of the time. Many of the animals the Egyptians worshipped had nothing obvious about them to make them divine. It is quite true that a good many of the wilder animals were gods, and it may look as though the more terrifying ones such as crocodiles were worshipped to keep them happy and placate their anger. For example, lionesses were connected with savage heat and desert winds and were symbols of pestilence and plague. Yet the Egyptians 'tamed' them by turning them into the lioness-headed Sekhmet, the patron goddess of doctors. Likewise the jackal, which scavenged graves and devoured corpses, was very much feared by the Egyptians who above all wanted their bodies to be undamaged. So they changed it from being an attacker into the protector of the dead, Anubis, the jackal-headed god of embalming. (This principle of 'placation' is well established in other cultures, too.

A mummified calf of the Roman period

The Greeks' name for the Furies who hounded people mercilessly was the 'Eumenides' or the 'favourably-disposed ones', and they named the Black Sea – infamous for its violent storms – the 'Euxine' or 'good to strangers').

But such a theory would not explain what the Egyptians found sacred about a frog or a baboon. Too literal an interpretation is misleading; in fact they acknowledged something sacred about *all* animals, because in animals they recognized a radical difference from themselves. Animals were not like human beings: they were not individuals who did stupid and wilful things to upset the flow of life. On the contrary, they represented the very continuity of nature – something which, as we have seen, the Egyptians revered above all else but from which, being human, they felt apart.

They therefore saw nature in terms of gods. Their everyday experience of the natural phenomena around them (birth, death, water, the seasons, their crops, the stars, etc.) turned their lives into a continuous relationship with their gods. It was this mystical and practical harmony of man and nature which gave the Egyptians their idea of divinity.

The Pharaoh

The person who ruled over this unchanging agricultural society was a god. The pharaoh's divinity was no mere metaphor: he had supernatural status since he was the successor of the creator himself who had been the first pharaoh of Egypt. In this way Egypt was not really a state or a country at all; it was the world itself, ordained by the creator and continuing to be ruled by him as part of the natural order. Everything came from the pharaoh: all power and wealth and authority, and there was no way of describing the land he ruled except as defined by the exercise of that power and wealth and authority. Remove the pharaoh (inconceivable thought!) and Egypt would vanish, lock, stock and barrel, together with all creation. 'What is the king of Upper and Lower Egypt? He is a god by whose dealing one lives, the father and mother of all men, alone by himself without an equal,' says Alan Gardiner in his translation of *The Autobiography of Rekhmire*.

Yet the pharaoh was no despot drunk with absolute power. He wielded justice or truth (*maat*) and it is most unlikely that the pharaonic system, had it led to arbitrariness and casual cruelty on a mass scale, would have lasted three thousand years without being overthrown. Indeed, the very stability of the system was both created and fulfilled by the Egyptians' expectation of changelessness. In this way the pharaoh was as much a part of the natural order as the animals they worshipped.

It has to be said, though, that after the chaos of the 1st Intermediate Period had been resolved and the Middle Kingdom had become established, the pharaoh's godlike status was never again quite what it had been in the Old Kingdom. From being quite literally untouchable by anybody other than close relatives (even accidental contact merited instant death) he gradually became 'humanized' so that by the New Kingdom he was a man among men enough to lead his troops on the battlefield or go hunting with his court. However, he retained his divine aspect at all times because mythology and the theory of the pharaonic system demanded it.

Death

As we said earlier, if the Egyptians acknowledged change at all it was only in the form of recurrent change like the seasons. Any other kind of change did not matter and could safely be ignored since it was only temporary. Even the death of a pharaoh was less than devastating because he never really died: he was born again in his own successor. However, this left the Egyptians with the awkward problem of how to accommodate their own deaths. As individuals they knew they were not going to recur like the seasons, and as commoners they knew they were not everlasting gods like the pharaoh.

They got round this problem by seeing death as an interruption to life which afterwards would continue 'elsewhere'. This way of dealing with death has been common among many different societies and at all times in history. But seldom has such emphasis been laid on taking the right number and variety of goods into the tomb in order to ensure survival after death. The burial treasures of the pharaohs are justly famous, and even the merely well-to-do took an extraordinary clutter of objects with them to their graves.

To judge from what they took it looks as though they were expecting life to go on exactly as before. But on closer examination this may be making too easy an assumption. A great part of their grave-goods were concerned directly or indirectly with providing themselves with food and drink, i.e. the means to go on living. Their tombs thus became intensive care units to keep their bodies going. This enabled that part of them which was not their bodies to live in an afterworld which, according to different myths, was by no means always identical to the world they had just left.

The KA

The Egyptians divided their 'spirit' (or whatever was not their physical bodies) into three separate entities. Firstly there was the *ka*, which was perhaps the nearest to what Protestant Christians would mean by the word 'spirit', and denoted a person's vital force or what made him a conscious being. In the plural, the word *ka* meant 'sustenance', clearly linking the spirit with its dependence on food. A dead man could be described as having gone 'to his *ka*'. Since his spirit had left his body but was presumed alive elsewhere it must obviously be getting nourishment from somewhere. Sustaining the *ka* after death was of prime importance to the Egyptians, which is why so many of their funerary rites were devoted to offerings of provisions. But all this was only a means to an end; the end was survival rather than the act of *ensuring* survival.

The *ka* did not have an individual existence of its own until after a person's death. It was then expected to inhabit the *ka*-statue in a chapel to which the offerings would be made, rather than live in the burial chamber itself, which might in any case be some distance away or deep underground.

The BA

Yet a man could not survive without a body. The idea of a person's disembodied *ka* living any sort of comprehensible life was alien to the Egyptians. The dead body had therefore to be well protected against the twin threats of decay and tomb-robbers. His *ka* and his preserved body were united into a new physical state which was able to leave the tomb and step out into the world of the living and was called the *ba*.

Ba means 'manifestation', and a dead person as represented by his *ba* could take on any shape he chose when leaving his tomb. Normally, however, the Egyptians pictured the *ba* as a bird with a human head. A translation of a text from the cenotaph of Seti I by Henri Frankfort in *Ancient Egyptian Religion* reads:

> These birds have faces like men, but their nature is
> that of birds. One of them speaks to the other with
> words of weeping. Now after they come to eat vegetables

Part of a cake, made from chopped dates, to be eaten in the after-life. From a New Kingdom tomb

The <u>ba</u> hovering over the mummy of Ani. It is one of the illustrations in Ani's Book of the Dead.

and green-stuff in Egypt, they flutter under the rays
of heaven and then their shapes become bird-like.

The Egyptians were always acutely conscious of the link
between the *ba*, which was privileged to be free to leave the
body, and the body itself which was home to the *ka*. The *ba* did
not have complete independence: the *ka* had first to be fed and
sustained, otherwise there could be no *ba*. At all events the *ba*
always returned to the tomb at night.

The AKH

The Egyptians held that the dead were dependent on their
tombs in order to live again as *bas* in a world which – if not
precisely like the one they had left – was nevertheless full of
everyday things and familiar to them from myth and legend.
But they also had a third concept, one which made the dead
person far more remote. This was the *akh*. It was a rarefied idea
to describe how the dead could be made part of the universe,
and thus immortal. The dead person's *akh* was that part of him

19

which dwelt among the stars rather than in an afterworld. There, in deep and glacial purity far removed from earth, the *akh* revolved slowly and majestically for ever around the North star Polaris.

It was with this idea of eternal life that the Egyptians managed to come to terms with the paradox of death. This paradox was that although death only ever came once to a person, it could hardly be dismissed as trivial along with everything else which did not recur. However, in the form of *akhu* they could, once dead, become part of the cosmos, endlessly and predictably revolving with the universe.

This spiritual trinity of *ka*, *ba* and *akh* which everyone possessed was quite a sophisticated solution to the common human difficulty of reconciling bodily death with the desire for an eternal life of some sort. By this means the Egyptians could have their cake and eat it: they could carry on living in a world directly linked to the one they had left (it was not only food that formed a link – people would write letters to their dead relatives asking for assistance) and at the same time they were assured of becoming part of the eternal universe. Yet this unfortunately led them straight into another awkward paradox. If a man in the form of his *akh* became an immortal part of the cosmos, and the pharaoh – being a god – was also part of the same everlasting order, did not that mean there was something in common between the pharaoh and the man? How could an Egyptian peasant have anything in common with a god? If such a thing could be, it would need a very convincing explanation.

Not surprisingly, the Egyptians found one. The solution lay in their legend of Osiris, probably the most famous piece of mythology ever to come from the ancient Near East.

The Osiris Myth

The myth of Osiris existed in various versions, depending on the period. Osiris gained in importance from the Old Kingdom and was pre-eminent by the Middle Kingdom. The legend itself, though, dates back in one form or another to pre-dynastic times. Unfortunately, the complete legend has never been found in an Egyptian source. There are numerous allusions to it throughout dynastic history, but it was evidently a tale too well known to have needed re-telling. It was up to the much later Greek writer Plutarch to piece together a full version.

According to the legend, Osiris was a just and good king who lived in the Nile Delta from where he ruled over all Egypt. For some reason his brother Set became insanely jealous of him and finally invited Osiris to a banquet given by his cronies. During the feast Set brought out a large and beautiful box which, he said, would be presented to whoever in the room fitted into it. One by one they all tried it, but it was not until Osiris lay down in it that the perfect fit was revealed. Promptly, Set's gang slammed the lid on him, fastened the catch, lugged him down to the Nile and threw him in. Thus Osiris was drowned.

His body was retrieved by his wife Isis but Set, on learning this, took it away from her and cut it up into fourteen pieces (or sixteen, depending on the version). He then scattered the pieces throughout Egypt. The grieving Isis, accompanied by her sister Nephthys, then trudged round Egypt looking for them, at last finding every bit except for her husband's penis.

This was no problem to someone with Isis's magic skills. She put Osiris together again so well that she conceived a son by him even though he was still technically dead. The son was named Horus and was kept hidden away in the Delta until he was old enough to take the throne and avenge his father's murder. It took a long time and many battles, but eventually Horus won and Set was soundly defeated.

The Osiris legend, like many including the Arthurian legend in Britain, was probably founded on fact. Many Egyptologists believe that there really *was* a king who, in pre-dynastic times, had ruled all Egypt from his capital in the Delta. The story of his violent death by drowning at the hands of his brother Set was probably an allegory to describe a rebellion from the southern city of Ombos which was later identified as the seat

A wall-painting from the tomb of Kynebu, showing Osiris with the four Sons of Horus before him on a lotus flower

of Set's worship. Osiris was presumably killed in this rebellion, and a war began which divided the country into two parts, Upper and Lower Egypt. When eventually Egypt was re-united, following a victory by the north, this was reflected in the Osiris legend by the account of Horus's victory over Set. The dead Osiris was then turned into a god. Seen in this way, the story is an allegory both of real historical events and of the age-old tale of good triumphing over evil. Isis was merely the personification of the throne (her name means 'seat'), and Nephthys represented Osiris's palace (her name means 'lady of the castle').

Legends arise not just because they are good stories but because they can be used to explain a culture's history or philosophy in a simple way. The Egyptians used Osiris himself to personify many things. From his drowning he became a vegetation god re-born after the annual Nile floods, and he also came to symbolize resurrection after his magical mending by his wife. This aspect of Osiris has special significance where the Egyptians' beliefs about death are concerned.

There was another side to Osiris, too, which gave this legend such power. Although he was pharaoh he was human. He was betrayed by his brother, murdered by his enemies, lamented by his wife and dependent on his son for revenge. He was therefore not the all-powerful, triumphant and immortal king but a betrayed and suffering figure. In this way the ordinary Egyptian could easily identify with him and hope that, if his own son could prove as reliable to him after death as Horus had to Osiris, he too could be re-born. (It is not difficult at this point to see common elements in the Osiris legend and Christian mythology). Thus bit by bit the Egyptians identified so closely with Osiris that they would refer to dead people as 'the Osiris so-and-so' or 'the Osiris x' just as we might talk about 'the late Mr Brown'.

But the Osiris myth was of still further use to the Egyptians since they could also employ it to describe and explain the pharaonic system. When a pharaoh died he became one with

Osiris, and his son Horus took the throne. The dead pharaoh, as Osiris, went back into the earth and became alive again with the Nile floods, the growing crops and the rising moon. Thus the long chain of pharaohs was nothing but the unchanging succession of Osiris and Horus endlessly repeated.

The Old Kingdom, which had seen the pyramid-building pharaohs at the greatest power they were ever to reach, was abruptly ended by the First Intermediate Period which temporarily plunged Egypt into anarchy. By the time unity was restored with the Middle Kingdom, Osiris had become useful once again. The system appeared to have broken down for a while, and the Egyptians badly needed a theory to explain how the great stream of Egyptian history was nevertheless still flowing as it always had despite a seeming interruption. They found one quite easily. In his rôle as a vegetation god, Osiris could be seen by all to be alive and well in the waving corn. In his rôle as a resurrection god, he was already identified with the imperishable dead pharaohs of olden days. The Egyptians had only to look at their crops to know that nothing had really changed. The new pharaohs of the Middle Kingdom were still one with the old: the system continued.

In this way the Osiris legend helped them make sense of the political turmoil from which they were emerging. It was typical that they should have looked backwards to an already ancient legend for an explanation rather than working out a new philosophy which could account for how their 'static' system had undeniably been given a bad shaking. In times of trouble, however, they reached for Osiris and with their extraordinary conservatism once more pressed him into service. He now became even more closely linked with resurrection and re-birth by guaranteeing the 'State's' immortality. Osiris was proved triumphant: the cosmic order was unshaken, Egypt's *akhu* were immortal; and since he was re-born as the current pharaoh, that same pharaoh's very existence guaranteed that the cosmic order was intact.

The Egyptians were thus employing a system of belief based,

like any religion, on a logical fallacy. In effect they were saying 'Egypt exists because Osiris exists, which proves Osiris must exist since Egypt does.' Given a philosophy as flexible as this, solving the problem of how ordinary mortals could have anything in common with a god was child's play. The Egyptians simply worked out that the Osiris x's *akh* could share the same universe with the pharaoh since both the universe and the pharaoh were also part of Osiris. It was a very neat solution.

In consequence Abydos, where Osiris's body was reputed to lie, became a popular place to be buried. And because of Osiris's oneness with the pharaohs the fashion grew for commoners to be buried with pictures of crowns, sceptres and other royal equipment on their coffins, a piece of democratization which would have been impossible in the grand old days of the Old Kingdom. But this identification with Osiris guaranteed the dead person's incorporation into the cosmic order. Whether his *akh* – according to his belief – went round with the stars, followed the sun, rose with the moon or, like Osiris, became one with the Nile and the crops, the ordinary Egyptian was assured of an eternal place in the cosmos. It was a triumph for mythology, theology, and sheer ingenuity.

The Universe

The Osiris myth explained well enough how Egypt was the universe (and therefore how the universe was Egypt), and it also explained the relationship between the universe, the pharaoh and the common people. However, like any ancient – or, indeed, modern – civilization, the Egyptians had their own version of how that universe had itself been created. They also had little stories to explain recurrent phenomena such as night and day and the appearance of the stars at evening.

Their story of creation was that the earth, Geb, and the sky, Nut, had given birth to the sun, Re. Each night Re was swallowed up again by Nut, passed through her body and was re-born again at dawn the next day. Geb, the earth, was thus the father of the gods, the most ancient of them all. This explanation of night was also adapted to account for the disappearance of the stars at dawn. The stars were in fact little piglets which a heavenly sow gobbled up when the sun rose and then gave birth to once again at sunset. The Egyptians' word for evening, *mesut*, actually means 'time of birth'.

But how had Geb and Nut themselves been created? This account of the birth of Re made a nice enough story of the day–night–day cycle, but it was much more of an illustration than an explanation. So the Egyptians devised a separate theory of creation. Awkwardly for us this theory never existed in a single form but was found in three main versions. These versions depended on where the story came from, since the three cities of Heliopolis, Hermopolis and Memphis each had its own tradition and each tradition was jealously guarded by its priests. Somewhat simplified, the different versions ran like this:

The Heliopolitan system

The world started with a chaos of shapeless masses of water called Nun. Out of Nun, self-created, emerged the sun Re (also at this point known as Atum), perched on a mound called a *benben* (see Chapter 4, p. 114). This creator god Re/Atum then produced Shu (air) and Tefnut (moisture) by a process of masturbation or spitting. Shu and Tefnut in turn produced Geb and Nut who themselves eventually created Osiris, Isis, Nephthys and Set. These nine (known to Egyptologists as 'the ennead') then governed Egypt by turn.

The Hermopolitan system

This theory also held that the world began with chaos, but it was a chaos made up of four constituents: water, space, darkness and invisibility, each of which had a male/female pair of gods. These eight gods (or 'the ogdoad') were represented as four couples of serpents and frogs, and together they created an egg on a mound which emerged from Nun at Hermopolis. Nun was thus the creator of Re/Atum, the sun.

The Memphite system

This system developed when Memphis became the Early Dynastic capital. Since Memphis was the seat of the god Ptah his priests insisted that he should play the leading role in the story of creation. Accordingly, Ptah took Re/Atum's place; but in order to avoid a direct confrontation with the priests at Heliopolis the Memphites compromised slightly. Ptah was still the great creator god but alongside him were eight other gods: Tatenen, the god of the earth emerging from chaos; Nun and Naunet (the first pair of the Hermopolitan ogdoad); Atum the great; and four others who were probably Horus, Thoth, Nefertum and some kind of a snake-god. Atum represented the creator god Ptah's intelligence and also his will. The intelligence was further personified by Horus, while the will was personified by Thoth.

According to this Memphite system Ptah first conceived the world intellectually before creating it. He then went on to the more mundane task of organizing civilization.

The Different Religions

Originally, there were two main branches of Egyptian religion: divine (the theology which accounted for the different gods and creation) and funerary, which was more concerned with death and the after-life. However, the more the Egyptians' civilization developed, the more they found they had to take into account the ancient popular beliefs which dated from way back before the priesthoods were formed. The divine and the funerary religions were understood only by the priests and the educated classes. The huge majority of Egyptians had their own beliefs, superstitions and local gods, depending on where they happened to live.

'Popular' divine religion

The animals of the animal cults were described on pp. 13–15 simply as gods, with only a general explanation of how they came to be so. In fact pre-dynastic Egypt had been split up into clans and tribes whose members believed their dead ancestors were reincarnated as animals or plants. In such animals and plants a divine power manifested itself which led naturally to the objects themselves being worshipped.

Later, many (but not all) of these primitive tribal gods became combined into single animals or objects which in turn became the 'patron' gods of the cities which were founded as the tribes settled down and united. Thus the pantheon of Egyptian gods grew and grew, although originally each city would only worship its own god. Moreover, they felt that each god had charge of a particular human emotion or natural phenomenon: thus Hathor, a cow, was goddess of love while Re, sometimes depicted as a ram, was the sun.

'Popular' funerary religion

As we have seen, the funerary part of Egyptian religion was of enormous importance, and the upper-class Egyptians devised their burials in the firm belief that the tomb would be needed by the dead person in his triple aspect of *ka*, *ba* and *akh*.

There was much more to funerary religion than this, though, since there were a great many theories and myths left over from the archaic and pre-dynastic civilizations, and the Egyptians hated above all to discard cherished old ideas. For example, there had always been a belief in the material survival of the soul near the tomb. But there was also a popular belief in life after death in a place called Amentit (the West) or in a place known as the Field of Rushes, a concept which harked far back to the idyllic pre-agricultural primeval landscape of the Nile Valley when the annual floods caused huge swamps in which rushes flourished. This belief was probably the oldest in Egyptian funerary religion. Both Amentit and the Field of Rushes were incorporated into Osirian doctrine and became very popular in the Middle Kingdom. The Egyptians regarded the West, where the sun sank, as its home; clearly Amentit was already part of the universe. The Field of Rushes, on the other hand, had to be given cosmic significance and this was done by making it one of the places in which the pharaoh might dwell in his solar afterlife. In addition to these two ideas there was also Duat, the underworld, which was a mirror-image under the earth of the living world lit by the sun on its overnight journey beneath the horizon.

'Priestly' divine religion

Side by side with these popular religious beliefs ran the religion of the intellectual élite, the priests. This, as we have seen, was more concerned with universal phenomena such as the rising and setting of the sun, the flooding of the Nile and all cyclical events without which the universe would have ground to a halt. This priestly religion resulted in physical objects such as temples, and in theological creations such as the cults, cosmogonies, sacrifices, offerings, 'enneads' and 'ogdoads', divine family triads and oracles. This whole mass of religious theory was sustained and added to by an ever more powerful clergy, who from the New Kingdom onwards constituted a separate social class.

State religion

As well as the popular and priestly religions, there was also what might be called the state religion although, as was explained earlier, the word 'state' is strictly inapplicable to ancient Egypt. This was the religion which stemmed from the pharaoh's divinity, a divinity which made him the only intermediary between the gods and mankind. Thus in theory he was the High Priest although in practice he had to delegate this rôle to others. The power of a particular state god varied, depending on whether he also happened to be the god of the ruling dynasty's native city. These state deities multiplied, but they never completely replaced each other. Neith, Set, Horus, Re and Ptah all waxed and waned in favour, but they all retained validity throughout dynastic Egypt.

While the priestly and the state religions developed more and more power and more and more sophisticated theologies, 'popular' religion also developed in its own way. The primitive cults' emphasis on magic became stronger until the Late Period when it prevailed. Popular religion then held its festivals on the same days as the state religion; it peopled the earth with demons and heroes such as Imhotep, the 3rd Dynasty royal architect (see Chapter 4); and it turned to magic and charms in time of trouble. It also had its so-called Mysteries, which were a repetition of dimly-remembered primordial rites that kept the universe going in much the same way as did the daily rituals of the priestly religion.

And finally, a kind of personal or private religion emerged with its own high moral and philosophical ideas of divinity.

The Legacy of Egypt

We know a considerable amount about a great many aspects of ancient Egyptian civilization partly because it was so long-lived and partly because it was literate and hence committed so much to writing. It is worth remembering that the pharaohs themselves were completely literate and were therefore not the mystified catspaws of the priests, which is rather more than may be said for a number of mediaeval monarchs. But it is a pity that so much of what has survived is concerned with death and the religious beliefs associated with death. Perhaps this is not surprising, given that the preservation of their tombs and bodies for eternity was the one thing to which they paid special attention. The most obvious relics of Egypt are huge stone monuments weighing thousands of tons and the imposing tombs of the rulers and the rich.

The impression is therefore of a civilization which was positively obsessed with dying, death, and a complicated array of gods and legends. Many writers have taken it upon themselves to describe this as a paradoxical reflection of the Egyptian people's great love of life, the idea being that they enjoyed it so much that they could not bear the thought of losing it. But this is sheer guesswork. It presumes a knowledge of a 'national character', whereas nearly all our available evidence concerns the customs and attitudes of royalty or the upper classes. It is all very well speculating about the origins of 'popular' religion in an anthropological way as we have just done; but there is little enough information on how the common people really thought or felt about anything – including life and death – since they were mostly illiterate and their thoughts have not survived.

In fact it is quite likely that the average Egyptian peasant was pretty hazy about his religious beliefs. He was no doubt highly superstitious and, depending on which dynasty he lived in, would reasonably have thought of the sun as being the most powerful and predictable phenomenon which ruled his world. Hence he might well have offered the sun an occasional prayer – either glum or gleeful, depending on the state of his crops. But as for the complex theology and cosmology which appears to us to have been so vital to everybody then, he would most likely have been quite ignorant about it, just as he would about ogdoads and enneads. He would have left all that sort of thing to his rulers: the pharaohs and the priests who could read and write the weird-looking inscriptions on their tombs. It was what the remote and the wealthy believed and had to do with power and riches and the splendid ceremony of state burials.

It is rather as if, in four thousand years' time, the remains of our present civilization in Britain were discovered, but practically the only things which had survived were cenotaphs, cathedrals and the records of Whitehall ministries. The people of A.D. 5978 would get a curiously lopsided view of what life in Britain had been like if all they had to go on were the remains of St Paul's and Westminster Abbey. There would be the tombs of statesmen, of kings and queens, of ponderous men of letters and dreary old admirals. And there would be all those texts carved in stone: snatches of the Bible and the Prayerbook, plus a quantity of third-rate poetry telling posterity that the fellow whose ancient bones lay beneath had once upon a time lived a good life.

It would all tend to give the impression that the average Briton of the late twentieth century had been obsessed with the

31

question of resurrection and that he was deeply committed to something called Christianity – one of the religions of that period. There would be no hint that millions of Britons lived their whole lives without much thought of religious observance and without going near a church except to be baptized, married or buried; and that if you had asked the famous man-in-the-street what the doctrine of the Trinity was he would probably have had no idea.

In all likelihood the man-in-the-street in Crocodilopolis or Thebes would have been similarly nonplussed if asked about the Osiris myth. He was happy to leave all that to the priests and the bigwigs, being much more concerned with the state of his emmer crop, the rising price of onions, his daughter's wedding or the worsening cracks in his bedroom wall.

So it should be remembered that what follows in this book is a description of the rituals mainly practised by a tiny minority of the Egyptian people, and that whenever 'the Egyptians' are referred to it means the people of that minority.

2

MUMMIFICATION

In a glass case in the public galleries of the Egyptian Antiquities Department of the British Museum there lies the body of a pre-dynastic (i.e. before 3100 B.C.) Egyptian. Because of his red hair he is known to staff and public alike as 'Ginger'. 'Ginger' is not a mummy: like countless other pre-dynastic Egyptians he was wrapped in skins or loose folds of linen and placed in a shallow grave on the edge of the desert where his body was quickly dried out by the hot sand. Today, 'Ginger' is merely skin and bone; yet even his finger- and toenails are perfectly preserved and he is recognizably a human being who ate, slept and walked more than five thousand years ago. When looking at him lying curled up on his left side it is difficult not to wonder what his relatives would have thought had they known when they heaped sand over him and piled rocks on top to prevent the jackals unearthing him, that after an inconceivable time and in an unheard-of place parties of tourists and school-children would shuffle round him as he lay in his case, pressing their noses against the glass and reflecting on how much would be left of their own bodies one day.

Could 'Ginger' himself have glimpsed the extraordinary future of his own mortal remains he might well have mistaken it for a proof that there was life after death. He and his people evidently believed in such a thing because they buried him with some black-topped red pottery vessels which once held food and drink for his long journey to the other world. Many

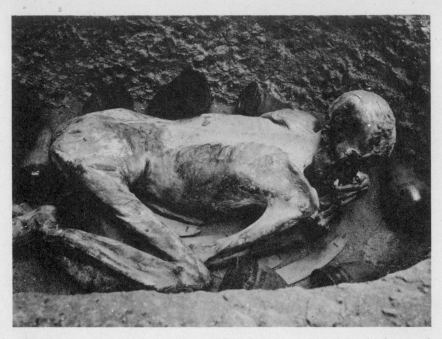

'Ginger', so-called because of his reddish hair, was buried in the hot sand around 3300 BC. He is remarkably well preserved and is on display in the British Museum.

other graves of this period contained jewellery, slate palettes on which to grind eye-paint, flint tools and combs of bone and ivory – all intended for use and enjoyment by the dead person in after-life.

Such early Egyptians must have been familiar with the effects on the body of burial in these shallow sand graves. No doubt they saw corpses which had been dug up by wild dogs and occasionally they themselves must have turned up an ancient cemetery by mistake. They would certainly have noticed that the bodies were quite well preserved. In fact, the corpses scarcely had time to putrefy. The intense heat of the sand would have drawn all the moisture out of the soft tissues, leaving them like tanned leather: gaunt and shrunken, perhaps, but having lost little other than the water which makes up 75% by weight of the human body.

It is impossible to tell now whether the lifelike appearance of their corpses actually caused the peasants of the Nile Valley to believe there was life after death, or whether it merely stimulated them further to produce the best possible preservation of their dead. However, not long after this period it is plain they must have believed that their 'spirits' would continue to need their physical bodies after death and therefore that they should be in as lifelike a state as possible.

We can deduce this because of what happened once the Dynastic Period began. The peasants would have continued the sand-burials for themselves, but for their rulers something a bit grander was required. A new burial fashion grew up for the pharaohs and the wealthiest. Chambers were now cut at the bottom of shafts deep underground and lined with stone, mud-bricks or wood. The bodies themselves were put in squarish wooden coffins and sealed up in these so-called *mastaba* tombs.

The Egyptians must quickly have discovered that this was disastrous. In their cool deep chambers the bodies no longer dried out: they grew damp and rotted until nothing but the bones remained. By this period there was a fairly clear theory about what happened to the 'spirit', and given that a dead person's *ka* and *ba* were dependent on his body, the early dynastic Egyptians must have been deeply concerned to find that the corpses of their pharaohs were putrefying. Aside from anything else, it upset so much theology.

At first they tried wrapping the bodies tightly with strips of bandage before putting them into the coffins in their hunched-up, foetal position; but by the 3rd Dynasty it was clear that whatever they did made not a scrap of difference. If such a body is unwrapped today it is inevitably found to consist of nothing but a jumble of bones inside a hollow shell of bandages. What has been preserved is a full-sized mould of the body; but the body itself has long since disappeared. There was no option, therefore, but to find an entirely new way of preserving bodies, and so the art of embalming began. It was an art which was practised from at least the early 4th Dynasty – Queen Hetepheres is the first known instance of mummification – right through Egyptian history until the early Christian and Coptic era: a span of some 2,700 years. During that time the quality of embalming practice varied considerably, but it reached its peak in about the 21st Dynasty (1085–945 B.C.).

Before describing the techniques it is necessary to explain that in this context 'to embalm' and 'to mummify' mean exactly the same thing. The word to embalm comes from the Latin *in balsamum*, which literally means to put into balsam – a mixture of various aromatic resins. As we shall see, this is not a completely inaccurate description since Egyptian corpses were indeed anointed with ointments, oils and resins. But the more usual word for an embalmed Egyptian body is 'mummy', and is the result of a simple mistake. Badly embalmed bodies of the Late Period were often so blackened and brittle that people believed they had been dipped in bitumen, the Arabic word for bitumen being *mumiya*.

Having no microscopes, the Egyptians were not to know that dead flesh decomposes through the action of bacteria and that there are three practical ways of preventing this in order to preserve a body after death:

(i) By refrigerating it.
(ii) By injecting antiseptic fluid into its veins and arteries so that the fluid gradually impregnates the surrounding tissues and prevents bacterial action. (This is the usual procedure nowadays and is simply a form of pickling.)
(iii) By drying the body out and then keeping it dry, bacteria needing moisture to thrive and multiply. The principle is identical to the South American cowboy one of 'jerking' beef.

Obviously, only the third course was open to the Egyptians. They already knew the hot top layer of desert sand dried the bodies out, but it also hardened them in a most un-lifelike way. The skin became a baked membrane stretched over the skeleton so that a fingernail flicked against it produced a sound like a wooden drum being rapped. This was clearly not quite what the *ka* and the *ba* would think of as home. What was needed was something besides external heat which would help dehydrate the bodies while leaving them reasonably flexible.

As it happened, Egypt possessed unlimited quantities of the ideal substance. This was natron, a naturally-occurring salt which in summer crystallized out as the small pools, left by the Nile floods, evaporated. The Egyptians called it *netjeryt* (i.e. divine or belonging to the god), and it can still be found plentifully, especially at Wadi el Natrun forty miles west of Cairo. The substance is a mixture of sodium bicarbonate (baking powder) and either sodium carbonate with sodium chloride (common salt) or sodium sulphate (Glauber's salt). Its chief property is that it is hygroscopic – that is, it absorbs moisture; but from the Egyptians' point of view it had the additional advantage of being mildly antiseptic.

They knew about these properties even in Old Kingdom times. In fact, they looked upon natron as a great purifying agent and chewed balls of it during certain religious rituals. It is from this period that Queen Hetepheres' burial dates. As has already been mentioned, hers is the first instance of mummification, although her body has not in fact survived. However, the embalmers removed her vital organs and put them in linen-wrapped packets in her Canopic box (see pp. 89–90) together with a 3% solution of natron. When this box was discovered and opened it was found to contain a liquid sludge which, after four thousand years, was all that remained of the Queen's insides.

The Egyptians reasoned that since putrefaction began in the abdomen they should first remove the insides and keep them separate. That way they could fill the abdominal cavity with natron so that the desiccation process could proceed simultaneously from outside and from within. However, it took them many centuries of trial and error, no doubt experimenting with solutions of every conceivable strength, to conclude that using natron in liquid form was not the answer. In point of fact

Embalmer's equipment and the ritual implements for the Opening of the Mouth ceremony. Left to right: Alabaster tray with model vessels and instruments for Opening the Mouth; pottery saucer with a linen bag containing natron; wax plate bearing the udjat-eye to cover embalmer's incision; wax figures of the four Sons of Horus; alabaster tablet naming the seven sacred oils used in the Opening of the Mouth ceremony; wooden mummy label with demotic inscription; wooden model adze used in the Opening of the Mouth ceremony

the Old Kingdom methods of mummification were not very efficient at all, which partly explains why not many mummies survive which can definitely be identified as belonging to this period.

Because the embalmers failed to stop all bacterial action their mummies went on decaying, although at a much slower rate. The embalmers therefore resorted to wrapping the bodies very tightly with resin-soaked linen bandages in order to preserve their original shape. The earliest mummy now in existence (the one in the Royal College of Surgeons in London was destroyed in an air-raid in 1941) is a good example of this. It is that of Waty, a court musician of the 5th Dynasty (c. 2400 B.C.) whose body was so expertly wrapped that his features are still perfectly recognizable beneath the bandages, down to the tiniest wart and wrinkle, including a callus on one of his feet.

Over the last century scholars have gradually built up a picture of the Egyptians' embalming process. The actual procedures varied a bit from one period to the next, but the principle remained much the same throughout two thousand seven hundred years: remove the insides, dry the body, re-pack it with stuffing to restore its original shape and wrap it up from head to foot.

By a stroke of luck we have an account of Egyptian embalming – possibly an eye-witness account – by a traveller in Egypt in the 27th Dynasty (about 450 B.C.). He was a Greek historian named Herodotus who was writing an enormous History of the known world. The whole of Book 2 of this History he devoted to Egypt and its customs; and although many of his stories and observations are dubious – not to say wildly exaggerated and malicious gossip he does provide an often very funny account of how a foreigner saw the world's oldest known civilization. His account of embalming is worth quoting in full, not least because it is so clear and matter-of-fact. He believes in no gods of any sort and so affects no bogus air of revealing unspeakable mysteries, for at this late period of Egyptian history embalming was quite simply a highly-developed commercial enterprise.

A papyrus, written in demotic script, of an embalmer's agreement

It was big business because a lot of money was involved; and just as today any funeral director will show you a range of coffins from cheap plain pine to expensive polished oak, so the Egyptian embalmers could offer their customers a choice of three styles as Herodotus describes:

Embalming is a distinct profession. The embalmers, when a body is brought to them, produce specimen models in wood, painted to resemble nature, and graded in quality; the best and most expensive kind is said to represent a being whose name I shrink from mentioning in this connexion [Osiris]; the next best is somewhat inferior and cheaper, while the third sort is cheapest of all. After pointing out these differences in quality, they ask which of the three is required, and the kinsmen of the dead man, having agreed upon a price, go away and leave the embalmers to their work. The most perfect process is as follows: as much as possible of the brain is extracted through the nostrils with an iron hook, and what the hook cannot reach is rinsed out with drugs; next the flank is laid open with a flint knife and the whole contents of the abdomen removed; the cavity is then thoroughly cleansed and washed out, first with palm wine and again with an infusion of pounded spices. After that it is filled with pure bruised myrrh, cassia, and every other aromatic substance with the exception of frankincense, and sewn up again, after which the body is placed in natrum, covered entirely over, for seventy days – never longer. When this period, which must not be exceeded, is over, the body is washed and then wrapped from head to foot in linen cut into strips and smeared on the under side with gum, which is commonly used by the Egyptians instead of glue. In this condition the body is given back to the family, who have a wooden case made, shaped like the human figure, into which it is put. The case is then sealed up and stored in a sepulchral chamber, upright against the wall. When, for reasons of expense, the second quality is called for, the treatment is different: no incision is made and the intestines are not removed, but oil of cedar is injected with a syringe into the body through the anus which is afterwards stopped up to prevent the liquid from escaping. The body is then pickled in natrum for the prescribed number of days, on the last of which the oil is drained off. The effect of it is so powerful that as it leaves the body it brings with it the stomach and intestines in a liquid state, and as the flesh, too, is dissolved by the natrum, nothing of the body is left but the bones and skin. After this treatment it is returned to the family without further fuss.

The third method, used for embalming the bodies of the poor, is simply to clear out the intestines with a purge and keep the body seventy days in natrum. It is then given back to the family to be taken away.

When the wife of a distinguished man dies, or any woman who happens to be beautiful or well known, her body is not given to the embalmers immediately, but only after the lapse of three or four days. This is a precautionary measure to prevent the embalmers from violating the corpse, a thing which is said actually to have happened in the case of a woman who had just died. The culprit was given away by one of his fellow workmen.

We now know that much of Herodotus's description is accurate, but certain parts need further explanation. One of the most vexed questions has been that of putting the body into natron. Some scholars used to believe that this meant soaking it in a natron solution, whereas others have pointed out that the word Herodotus uses is the one the Greeks always used to describe their own method of drying fish by packing them in salt. For some time Egyptologists were divided into those who favoured the soaking theory and those who favoured the dry packing. It now seems that the latter were right, partly for theoretical reasons and through the re-examination of existing material, but also because one or two investigators had the wit to put the matter to the test.

An Egyptologist named Lucas decided that the way to settle it was to see what happened if you soaked plucked dead chickens and pigeons in natron solution and then compared the results with those obtained by covering them with dry natron. He had always thought that the soaking theory was unlikely – for the good archaeological reason that the Egyptians would have needed a great many baths or vats to steep the bodies in and nothing like that has ever been found. Whereas if the other theory were right the bodies would simply have been lain on mats on the ground with piles of natron heaped over them. (This would also conveniently explain why many mummies are incomplete or damaged; had they been on the ground they would have been fair game for the pariah dogs and jackals which would have slunk in by night from the edge of the desert.) Lucas's experiments with his chickens and pigeons indicated clearly that dry natron had to have been used. One of the reasons advanced in favour of the steeping theory had been that many mummies have their toe- and fingernails tied on or capped with little metal thimbles. This, said some people, was to stop them coming off as they tend to if bodies are soaked in water for any length of time. But Lucas discovered that dry packing with natron will produce the same effect, particularly if the body is already beginning to decay.

The other point which his experiments established was that of the time taken to dehydrate the body. Herodotus gives seventy days, but Lucas found this was far too long. In fact Herodotus must have misunderstood his informant because seventy days was the length of time the entire embalming process usually lasted, including removal of the intestines and wrapping. The dehydration itself took forty days, which interestingly ties up with the description in the Old Testament of the deaths of Jacob and Joseph (Genesis ch. 50), both of whom were mummified. Jacob's embalming is definitely described as having taken forty days. Since Lucas found that seventy days' steeping would bring off the body's limbs there is no doubt that Herodotus was wrong about this – and the claim at the entrance to the tomb of the 4th Dynasty Queen Meresankh III that she took two hundred and seventy-two days to embalm is clearly referring to the entire process from death to burial, including all sorts of religious rituals and ceremonies. It reads: 'ist Year, ist month of summer, day 21, her *ka* rested, she went to the *wabt* [see p. 44]. 2nd Year, 2nd month of spring, day 18, she went to her beautiful tomb.'

Lucas's experiments have more recently been confirmed by Dr Zaki Iskander in Cairo who reached the same conclusions by experiments with dead animals. We are now in a position to describe in some detail the main stages of embalming as practised by the ancient Egyptians.

Not long after death (in that climate presumably only a day or two: the reason for delay which Herodotus gives may have been true, but since he was a Greek he might have invented it about the Egyptians as a scurrilous piece of scandal-mongering) the body was taken first to the *ibu*, the place of purification, then to the *wabt*, the place of embalming, or there was the *pr-nfr* which probably combined both functions. There the body was undressed and placed on a large wooden embalming table.

The face and head were the priorities since in Egypt's heat, putrefaction would have set in quite quickly and it was important to preserve the features before they were affected by decomposition. The embalmers probably first washed the whole body with a natron solution, and in addition gave the face a thin coat of hot resin. They were then ready to remove the brain. Up to the 18th Dynasty this was rarely done because the Egyptians seem not to have thought the brain of any importance; according to them it was the heart that was the seat of a person's intelligence. But from the 18th Dynasty onwards it became standard practice, certainly in the most expensive kind of embalming.

The brain was removed by putting a chisel up the left nostril and breaking through the sinus into the skull, or occasionally they went through the side of the head just behind the left eye. Then they inserted a piece of stiff wire with a hook which they stirred around to cut the brain into pieces, and spooned the fragments out by means of another rod with a little cup-shaped end. Clearly, this was quite a violent process and there was some risk of damaging the features. Very occasionally, as in the cases of King Ahmose and Waty, the embalmers trepanned the skull – that is, they cut a hole in the back of the head and removed the brain that way.

Because they thought it unimportant, the Egyptians never preserved the brain like the other organs. When the skull was empty they sometimes left it like that, but generally they filled it with resin or sawdust or resin-soaked linen.

The face and head having been dealt with, the next move was to take out the entrails. Another Greek historian, Diodorus Siculus, provides a strange detail at this point which Herodotus

Waty – the oldest known mummy in the world, in the tomb of Nefer at Saqqara c. 2400 BC

does not mention. It seems that an embalmer called 'the scribe' first drew a mark on the left side of the abdomen. Then a colleague named 'the ripper-up' made an incision along the mark before taking to his heels while the other embalmers hurled stones and curses after him. If such a thing did happen, then it must have been of purely ritual significance, no doubt a relic of some religious law which forbade injuring dead bodies. Herodotus's description suggests a rather more leisurely scene; but the 'flint knife' – which was used for religious rituals like circumcision – does imply that the whole of the embalming operation was itself a religious ritual involving certain archaic procedures which may have dated back to early Egyptian history.

In any case, once the abdomen had been opened the embalmers presumably felt that whatever else they did to the body would not make matters worse. Which was just as well, because their next step was to put a hand in through the cut and pull out the stomach and intestines. They then washed the abdomen out before puncturing the diaphragm and removing the con-

45

tents of the chest, leaving only the heart behind. Usually they had also left the kidneys in the abdomen; but cases are known in which everything was removed, just as there are one or two instances in which all the viscera were left intact. But the heart was generally left in place because it was somehow connected with the seat of intelligence and the will.

There was an alternative method, mainly used in the cheaper forms of embalming, of clearing out the viscera. This was the one Herodotus mentions involving a rectal injection of 'cedar oil' which would dissolve the internal organs. However, modern writers like Lucas are a bit sceptical about this. The 'cedar' would probably have been a species of juniper; but in any case it would not have had such an effect all on its own. Lucas believes that if the body were dried with natron but with the viscera still inside then the natural process of decomposition would have turned the viscera into a thick liquid, especially if some of the natron solution had found its way into the body. It is quite likely that Herodotus mistakenly attributed this effect to the juniper oil.

Then the abdomen and chest cavity were rinsed out with spices and palm wine. The spices were probably used more as a deodorant than for anything else. One has to remember that all this was taking place in a hot country some thousands of years before refrigeration was invented, and that the body would probably not have been fresh to begin with. No matter how much the Houses of Embalming and Purification were sluiced out with water and disinfected with bucketfuls of natron, the smell would surely have been appalling.

Imagine a hall with several large tables like wooden fish-monger's slabs, each with a corpse on it in a different stage of embalming and decomposition, and each with its attendant team of embalmers. The floor would be running with water. Somewhere out at the back would probably be a large shed in which the bodies were stacked in racks or lain on the ground, covered in natron for the forty days' dehydration. If an epidemic were raging the embalmers would be working hard to clear a backlog of dead bodies which were not getting any sweeter while they waited.

Almost certainly the hall would have echoed the noise of chatter punctuated with loud outbursts of laughter. Yet this would hardly be surprising, since although the age-old procedure of mummification held religious significance, the embalmers themselves were merely doing a job of work, and like anybody engaged in macabre or unpleasant occupations they would probably have acquired a kind of gallows-humour to carry them through. The jokes and stories would doubtless have cheered up a gruelling day's work as the sun climbed, the heat increased, the smell got worse, the flies came in black swarms and still further trade was announced by relays of grieving relatives. Sweating boys would have trotted about with vessels of water and baskets of fresh natron. Some would have pushed brooms continuously up and down the alleyways between the tables, keeping the water on the floor moving and edging any rubbish towards the door, while others would have gone about scattering handfuls of natron which scrunched underfoot like gravel. Still younger boys would have been employed to throw stones at the dogs which nosed around the door or came slinking round the back too close to the drying-shed.

When the embalmers had removed the entrails they washed them and put them into natron to dry for forty days or thereabouts. At the end of that time they were removed, dressed with some sort of scented oil and molten resin before being carefully wrapped in linen into neat bundles. These bundles were then placed in four canopic jars (see pp. 89–91) for burial with the body. (There were variations to this. In the 21st Dynasty the bundles were replaced inside the mummy, and in the 26th they were packed between its legs.)

Next, the body itself had to be dried. The natron-and-sunshine treatment left it little more than a skeleton draped with loose folds of skin: most of the muscle and soft tissues were completely dissolved or broken down. To prevent disfigure-

Canopic jars for holding the embalmed viscera. These limestone jars were made for Nesi-Khonsu, wife of the High Priest of Amun Pinodjem. Their stoppers represent the heads of the four Sons of Horus. Baboon-headed Hapy looked after the lungs; Duamutef, who had a dog or a jackal's head, protected the stomach; human-headed Imsety guarded the liver and Qebhsenuef, with his hawk-head, watched over the intestines.

ment as well as to hurry the drying-out process the empty abdomen and chest were packed with temporary stuffing. For this the embalmers used whatever came to hand: rags, sand, wood shavings, straw, resin, dried grass – anything would do.

Then the body was put on a mat or, better, lain on a sloping board so that any seepage could drain away, and covered with heaps of natron. This drying-out took up to the forty days' maximum, or roughly half Herodotus's estimation.

At the end of this time the embalmers would remove the body, which by now would have been a fairly horrific sight. It would have changed colour, going much darker, and would be anything up to 75% lighter in weight. The legs and arms would have dwindled to matchsticks sleeved in loose, rather rubbery, skin, while the stuffed abdomen would have looked taut and out of proportion. This stuffing would then have been taken out and put on one side while the body was washed and dried.

Now the empty head was stuffed if it had not already been done. Linen swabs soaked in resin were pushed up into the cranium via the hole through which the brain had been extracted. The chest and abdomen were then re-stuffed, usually with the same resin-soaked linen but later with rather more informal materials such as sawdust in the case of Ramesses V or lichen as with Ramesses IV. The wound in the abdomen was then closed. It was sometimes sewn, and not always very well either. There are plenty of mummies whose incisions look as if they had been roughly tacked together with a carpet-needle and thin string: huge ragged stitches more suitable for Frankenstein's monster than for a pharaoh. Instead of stitches, though, the Egyptians often used a piece of gold foil or a tablet of beeswax bearing the symbol of the *udjat* eye (see p. 83) which they kept in place by pouring molten resin over it.

The embalmers then rubbed the whole body with a lotion of juniper oil, beeswax, spice and natron.

The nose was plugged, and wads of linen were also pushed up into the sunken cheeks in an attempt to counteract the withered appearance which the drying-out caused. This stuffing must have done much to restore some lifelikeness, but the embalmers occasionally overdid it. Queen Henttawy (21st Dynasty) was overstuffed, and she now presents a grotesque spectacle since her cheeks have burst. Clearly, she had not been thoroughly desiccated before burial and the flesh of her face had dried still further, shrunk over the linen wads and cracked with the strain.

At this stage the eyes were also dealt with. They were not taken out, but pushed down into their sockets and covered with little pads of the resinated linen. The eyelids were then pulled down over the pads. In the 21st Dynasty artificial eyes with painted pupils were slipped over the real eyeballs. These false

49

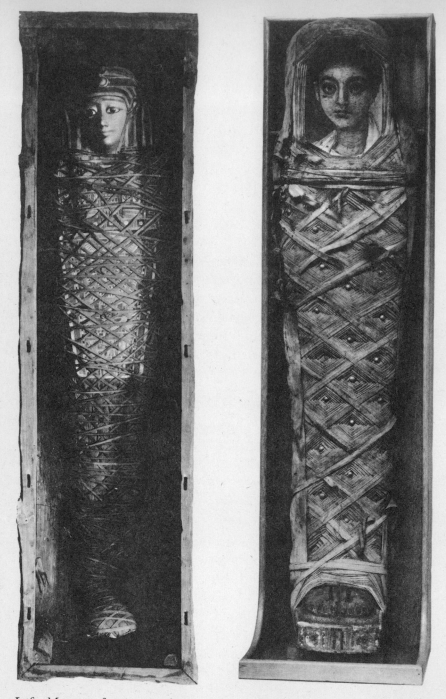

Left: Mummy of a man wearing a cartonnage mask and pectoral, tightly bound with linen strips. Right: Mummy of a boy from the Roman period with a painted portrait panel incorporated into his very decorative wrappings

eyes were usually made of something like alabaster, and in such cases the eyelids were left open. Then the embalmers checked over the rest of the body to see if any parts needed stuffing to make the whole more lifelike. In the 21st Dynasty they quite frequently packed mud or sand under the skin through fresh incisions, and in the worst examples they used old rags, sawdust and even twigs.

Finally, the embalmers painted the entire body with molten resin. The idea of this was to toughen the skin and make it waterproof. They now went over the waterproofed body with cosmetics, touching up here and there, adding a bit of colour or painting in an eyebrow. Often they painted the face – and sometimes the whole body – with ochre: red for men and yellow for women. After this they put on any jewellery with which the dead person was to be buried, and then they were ready for the last, and perhaps most exacting, step: that of wrapping the mummy.

This proceeded with many prayers and rituals and therefore took up a good deal of time. Yet in terms of preserving the body's lifelikeness it was time well spent, since it was the care with which they wrapped it, the tightness and the stiffness of the bandaging, which would maintain its detail and shape.

They began by wrapping the fingers and toes separately. After each finger and toe they went on to each limb; and when the limbs were finished the mummy-mask was placed over the head and shoulders. Then followed one or more shrouds held in place by some bandages stretched lengthwise and across.

As they wrapped the corpse, so the embalmers placed various amulets and sometimes the *Book of the Dead* papyrus (see pp. 88–89) among the bandages. It is not unusual with mummies of the 20th–22nd Dynasties to find dried onions among the bandages as well. They must have had some special significance because they are also found in coffins, in the mummy's pelvis and chest, stuffed into its ears and in one case bandaged over its eyes.

After the peak of embalming was passed in the 21st Dynasty, the art of treating the actual body declined, and the real care

Mummy of a man, found in the coffin of a New Kingdom woman called Mutemmenu. He is very skilfully bandaged – each finger and toe has been separately and elaborately wrapped.

and skill was transferred to the bandaging which became more and more elaborate. From quite late on, in the Ptolemaic and Roman periods, there are many indifferently-embalmed mummies which have been beautifully and intricately bandaged. Since the wrapping of mummies became an art in itself there are many from this period which have never been unwrapped. They are X-rayed to see if there are any particularly interesting objects or amulets on the body, and then left as outstanding examples of the bandagers' art.

Once the wrapping of the mummy was complete, the embalmers were ready to hand the dead person back to the relatives for burial. Meanwhile, they had gathered together every single thing which had come into contact with the body during the process of embalming over the previous weeks. This included soggy packs of natron, all the temporary stuffing materials, rags, swabs and any bits and pieces like fingernails that may have sloughed off during the natron treatment. All this was put into sixty-seven pots to be buried near the tomb. This was necessary because the Egyptians believed that if an enemy got hold of so much as a single hair it could be used to bewitch them. It was also clear that when the dead person awoke in the afterlife he would need his body as it had been when alive, and not with little pieces missing; yet the putrid swabs were obviously unclean and so could not be allowed into the tomb itself.

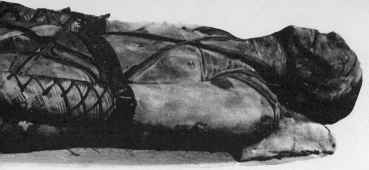

There was now nothing more to be done except for the friends and relatives of the deceased to bury him according to the proper rituals (see next chapter). In all, the whole embalming would have lasted some seventy days, and much of this time would have been spent after the natron treatment on the slow process of the wrapping.

The practice of embalming continued in Egypt until the third or fourth century A.D.; but with the exception of the intricate geometrical patterns which characterized bandaging under the Romans, it was a pale shadow of the art it had once been. A very crude form of embalming lingered on, practised by the Copts and early Christians, until A.D. 641 when the Arab era began and it finally stopped entirely.

The condition of the mummified bodies which have survived varies enormously. Many of them are merely bones contained in a hard shell of bandages. Others, like that of Waty and certain of the Deir el Bahri royal mummies, are perfectly preserved in form. Some, especially those from the later dynasties and Ptolemaic period which have been completely eviscerated and filled with molten resin, are well preserved but quite hard and black. After such a long time the resin seems to have penetrated the bones themselves so it becomes quite difficult to tell which is bone and which resin. The entire body appears to be made of solid bitumen, hence the misnomer of 'mummy'. Even Wallis Budge was misled by this, although in his book

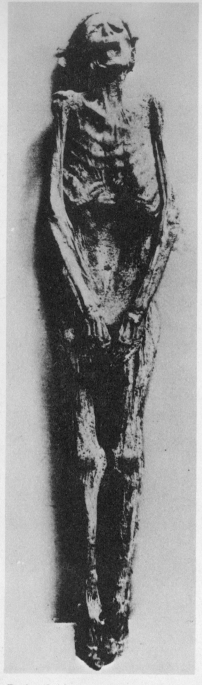

Body of an unnamed prince from the
royal cache of mummies at Deir el
Bahri. It is thought he either died in
convulsions as a result of poisoning,
or that he was buried alive.

Unwrapped mummy of
an elderly woman

The Mummy he does describe quite vividly the effects of this embalming technique:

> The arms, legs, hands, and feet of such mummies break with a sound like the crackling of chemical glass tubing; they burn very freely, and give out great heat. Speaking generally they will last for ever.

He goes on to discuss the specific effect of the natron treatment:

> When a body has been preserved by natron . . . the skin is found to be hard, and to hang loosely from the bones in much the same way as it hangs from the skeletons of the dead monks preserved in the crypt beneath the Capuchin convent at Floriana, in Malta. The hair of such mummies usually falls off when touched.

Other mummies, such as those of Yuya and Thuya (the parents of Queen Tiye, 18th Dynasty), are beautifully preserved – so much so that it is perfectly easy to imagine them alive. The features of such mummies are often so detailed that they can be of great help to Egyptologists in deciding whether certain people were related to each other. Family resemblances, such as a particularly long chin or straight nose, have sometimes helped solve genealogical puzzles where the records are missing or unclear.

On the other hand, some mummies pose fresh mysteries rather than help to clear up old ones. An example of this is the so-called 'unmummified mummy' which was found at Deir el Bahri amongst the Royal cache in a plain white mummy case without the usual beard and without any name or inscription. This anonymous body was wrapped in a sheepskin, which was itself curious since Herodotus reported that the Egyptians believed wool too unclean to be taken into temples and tombs. This is confirmed by a passage in *The Story of Sinuhe* (included in Adolf Erman's *The Literature of the Ancient Egyptians*) in which King Sesostris I recalls Sinuhe from abroad:

> Thus you will not die abroad, nor will the Asiatics bury you.

You will not be placed in a sheepskin . . . So think of your dead body and return.

How it was unwrapped is best described by a Frenchman named Mathey who was present and watching with considerable interest. His report is dated Cairo, 15 November 1886:

Once the bandages had been stripped off we found the mummy was encased in a sort of whitish material rather like dough which was extremely caustic and covered the body from head to toe at an average thickness of between 0.10 and 0.15 centimetres. At this moment we all had to overcome a sense of utter revulsion. Besides the repulsive smell caused by the release of noxious gases which had been trapped inside, the salty substance which formed this dough was strongly hygroscopic; once in contact with the air it rapidly absorbed moisture. Those unwrapping the mummy had therefore to remove this thick coat piece by piece. Finally, though, thanks to their skill the mummy emerged intact.

It is difficult to give an accurate description of the expression of the face thus laid bare. I can only say that no countenance has ever more faithfully recreated a picture of such affecting and hideous agony. His features, horribly distorted, surely showed that the wretched man must have been deliberately asphyxiated – most probably by being buried alive. There is evidence to back up such a dramatic theory, too. The body was buried without the usual embalming: the brain had not been extracted and all the viscera and internal organs were intact. The limbs were also tightly bound, arms straight down at the sides and feet together without the slightest bend in any joint. I can only think of two possible theories to fit these facts: firstly that the man had been buried alive or, secondly, that he had died of convulsions due to having taken poison.

The mummy is that of a male, seemingly between 25 and 30 years old, well built and apparently without any wounds or marks on his body. In general he is perfectly preserved,

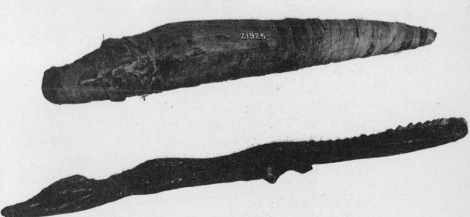

Left: Mummified dog and jackal, sacred animals of the god Anubis or Wepwawet. Below: Wrapped and unwrapped crocodile mummies, sacred to the god Sobek

for all that he is extremely parchment-like and of a deep mahogany colour.

This mummy is indeed a grim sight. It is true that he had not been embalmed in the proper way, but there had been some attempt at preservation because there was natron between the layers of bandages and packs of natron next to the skin. It looks as though his arms and legs were originally twisted in agony, just as his stomach is painfully contracted, but that the embalmers straightened them out with difficulty and kept them in place with tight bandaging. His head is thrown back, his mouth frozen open in a lopsided gasp. When on closer inspection it was found that there *was* physical damage, contrary to what M. Mathey said, it was suggested that the unknown wretch had been impaled on a sharpened stake. Then it appeared more likely that the damage was caused by his embalmers; and since he undoubtedly died in convulsions a theory arose that the embalmers had begun their treatment while he was still alive.

Whatever the no-doubt-horrid truth, this anonymous body does suggest one possibility which also fits with other facts. For a start, it was found in a Royal cache, which makes the young man a prince at least. But a prince would surely have been accorded proper embalming – unless, of course, he had been in some kind of unforgiveable disgrace.

From papyri we learn that in the reign of Ramesses III (20th Dynasty) there was a conspiracy to kill the King, and following the trial it seems that the most important members of the plot were allowed to commit suicide rather than suffer the indignity of execution. If so, was this unknown young prince one of those plotters who failed to overthrow his own father and was forced in consequence to take poison? We shall no doubt never know for certain; but the mummy is of exactly the right period and the theory fits the known facts quite neatly. Too neatly, perhaps. The real explanation might have been far less glamorous, but it was probably forgotten not long after they wrapped him up in his insulting sheepskin shroud.

Above: Two mummified hawks bandaged together. The hawk was the sacred bird of Horus. Right: Wooden cat coffin, the head painted to imitate a bronze mask

Two mummified cats either side of a mummified ibis. Cats were sacred to Bastet, the ibis to Thoth.

The close scientific examination of mummies has enabled us to discover many things about the Egyptians which otherwise would have remained unknown, such as the diseases they suffered from and the difference between the everyday diet of the rich and the poor. Some of these findings will be discussed more fully in the last chapter of the book. Meanwhile, it is enough to say that where mummies are concerned one does not have to be a scientist to perceive details that bring these long-dead people touchingly close. Some of the bodies resume their decay as soon as they are unwrapped, showing that there is still enough of their original organic remains to putrefy. Others still smell powerfully of the spices they were embalmed with. The mummy of Amenophis I (an 18th Dynasty king) had been battered by tomb-robbers not long after his death, and when he was re-wrapped by 21st Dynasty priests they included some delphiniums among his bandages. When he was moved from his case in Cairo a few years ago the whole room was suddenly flooded by the pungent scent of the three-thousand-year-old delphiniums. He has been left wrapped because of the excellent bandaging and amongst the garlands around his neck is a preserved wasp.

The Egyptians apparently used other methods of embalming, though. Alexander the Great, who was Egypt's first Macedonian king (following on the 30th and the last native dynasty) was reputedly embalmed in honey. He lay in a glass case in Alexandria so that the curious could go and see him submerged in his sticky tomb. The Arab historian Abd el Latif (A.D. 1162–1231) reported that he had been told 'by an Egyptian worthy of belief' about a party of treasure-seekers who were poking about the pyramids when they came across a sealed jar. They opened it, found it was full of honey, and sat down to have it for lunch. One of the party, dipping his bread into it, found a hair which he pulled. More and more hair emerged from the honey, followed by the body of a small child perfectly preserved. It was apparently well-dressed and decked out with ornaments, but even this cannot have done much to restore their appetites.

It was not only human beings the Egyptians embalmed. As we saw in Chapter 1 nearly every animal known to them had some religious significance. Mummies survive of practically every beast: mummy birds, mummy cats, mummy dogs, mummy fish and even mummy snakes. Perhaps the most celebrated of all mummified animals are the Apis Bulls of Memphis.

There was only one Apis bull at any given moment, and it was found by scouring Egypt for a male calf that was exactly the right colour, had precisely the right markings and scrupulously fulfilled various other religious and astrological stipulations. These made the right calf sacred, and from then on it was treated like a pharaoh for life, with priests and servants ministering to what they interpreted as its whims. They even supplied it with a harem of hand-picked cows for its pleasure.

Right: Granite sarcophagus of an Apis bull in the Serapeum at Saqqara. Below: Alabaster embalming table for the Apis bull in the temple of Ptah at Mit Rahina, site of Memphis

When the Apis bull died the Egyptians embalmed it with all the care otherwise reserved only for kings and nobles. To mummify a large bull was clearly quite a task, and the huge alabaster tables that were used have recently been found at Memphis near the Temple of Ptah. When the mummy bull was ready it was buried with great ceremony in the Serapeum, a vast catacomb in the Saqqara necropolis, and enclosed in a stone sarcophagus which sometimes weighed more than sixty tons. (See also pp. 73, 75.)

The mummy of Maat-ka-re provided another curiosity. Maat-ka-re was a 'god's wife', a priestess who had also to be a virgin. She was buried with a much smaller mummy which for years was believed to be her child and which presumably meant that she had died in childbirth. This naturally made it impossible for her to have been a virgin and so there was a good deal of speculation about the degree of licence allowed to the wives of gods until somebody thought of X-raying the little mummy. Her 'child' turned out to be a mummified baboon, probably her favourite pet.

Apart from pets, though, most animals were mummified as part of the religious industry which flourished in Ptolemaic and Roman times. Entire cemeteries were reserved for particular kinds of animals and were near the centres of the appropriate cults. The cat-cemeteries were at Bubastis, the centre of worship of the cat-goddess Bastet, and there is a large ibis-cemetery at Hermopolis in honour of Thoth, the ibis-headed god. Besides the Apis bulls at Saqqara there are also in the catacombs there hundreds of thousands of conical pots containing the mummies of ibises and hawks. It used to be the practice for visitors to the catacombs and their accompanying shrine to buy a mummy and dedicate it to the god in return for a favour, just as some Roman Catholics will buy a candle to put in front of the statue of a saint in the hope of having a prayer answered. However, some of these 'mummies', when unwrapped, have been found to contain not birds but bunches of twigs, pieces of linen and sawdust; evidently some of the religious mummy-sellers of those days were operating a racket akin to that which, one thousand years later, had holy men going round Europe selling pieces of 'the True Cross'. Indeed, the manufacture of fake mummies eventually became big business, as we shall see in the last chapter.

3

FUNERARY EQUIPMENT

As was noted in the first chapter, we unfortunately have very little idea of how the average Egyptian thought or what his religious beliefs were. What we do have are the relics of rituals which the Egyptian upper classes – and later the middle class – acted out to ensure their survival after death. It is never easy to separate ritual from belief; it is conceivable that after the early dynasties many Egyptians observed their burial customs not because they positively believed in them but because they feared to discard them.

It is important to remember that when people refer to the burial customs of the Ancient Egyptians they imagine that they are talking only about royalty. They have in their mind's eye an image of pharaonic splendour – of priceless possessions and gold by the hundredweight – and assume that only the kings of Egypt were buried in such style. Yet in fact the entire Egyptian upper class aspired to a ceremonial State burial; and the interment of minor members of the royal family, of high priests, of court scribes, of army generals and provincial governors was often scarcely less splendid than that of the Pharaoh himself.

Originally, the status of a god which the king had enjoyed in the early dynasties had led him to be accorded the most lavish burial money could buy. But bit by bit, as the sole might of the pharaoh became compromised by the rising power of priests, courtiers and gentry, and as Egypt's wealth increased and found its way into more hands, other people could afford for themselves the sort of burial which had once been exclusive to kings. This process went on throughout Egyptian history, so that by the late dynasties successful merchants and trades-people had adopted for themselves many of the rites which had begun as suitable for gods. They might not have been able to afford the lavishness of the kings, they might not have been able to muster pounds of gold, silver and bronze to take with them into their tombs; but they could and did adopt the rites and customs.

A good example of this is the way in which the pyramid was originally the tomb of a great ruler such as Khufu (Cheops), but fifteen hundred years later had shrunk from an engineering feat to a little model surmounting most middle-class tomb chapels. Similarly, although the funerary objects and customs described in this book originally applied only to pharaohs, they quickly became widespread among the rich and powerful at the upper end of Egyptian society, and many of them eventually became common property.

Probably most Egyptians had some idea of an after-life in which they would go on doing much the same things as they always had, except in rather better conditions. If they were farmers, then the sun would never be quite so viciously hot; the Nile would always flood on time and always in the right amount; they would have bumper harvests year after year for the rest of time; their donkeys would never wear out and drop dead – any more than their wives, who would merrily go on bearing them an infinite succession of bonny sons.

Even the pharaohs thought along similar lines. Because agriculture in the Nile Valley was central to the wealthy Egyptian economy, the pharaohs could not imagine an after-life in which agriculture was not the main occupation. Even though in real life a pharaoh would never have done a stroke of such work and would probably have died of shock if it had been suggested that he might like to take a sickle out one afternoon for a little light reaping, there are nevertheless illustrations in the *Book of the Dead* which depict queens actually cutting corn and one representation on a temple wall of a king ploughing and reaping.

But whatever your status on earth, participation in the afterlife depended, the Egyptians believed, on three basic things. Firstly, your body must be kept intact; secondly, your name should continue to exist; and thirdly you must be kept supplied with food and drink. To guarantee these three the Egyptians took into their tombs with them a great quantity of practical and symbolic items and equipment.

> (i) Keeping the body intact was a matter of correct embalming and burial procedure, the body being well wrapped and placed in a nest of coffins which were finally protected by a heavy sarcophagus. It was also a matter of including with the wrappings a series of magic charms, among them *amulets* and *scarabs*. On papyri or inside the coffin would be written selections from the famous Egyptian collection of spells, the *Book of the Dead*.
>
> (ii) Ensuring that your name would last was a comparatively simple matter. It was carved, written or painted just about anywhere convenient: on your possessions, your coffins, your sarcophagus, your tomb walls.
>
> (iii) Guaranteeing your supply of food and drink for your journey through the other world was a question of taking with you the necessary practical equipment (sickles, hoes and other tools) and/or the right symbolic equipment such as *shabtis* and wooden models.

Much of the above, especially the words in italics, needs explaining, and *shabtis* are a good place to start.

Shabtis of various styles and periods dating from the Middle Kingdom to the Ptolemaic period

Shabtis

The Egyptian ruling caste wished to make quite certain that nothing like agricultural labouring would spoil their after-life of ease and plenty. They did not much like the idea of an eternity spent ploughing and sowing, so it was essential for them to have this taken care of. What they needed was a way of guaranteeing an adequate supply of servants to do the dirty work for them, and so they took into their tombs with them little figurines called *shabtis*. So far as we know, *shabtis* started off in the Middle Kingdom as statuettes shaped like mummies representing the mummy of the dead person they accompanied. The idea seems to have been that if anything happened to the actual body, the models could act as a substitute home for the *ba* which would otherwise have been left homeless. The Egyptians already had a system of so-called 'reserve heads': they were buried during the Old Kingdom with models of their own heads which could deputize if anything happened to the real one, and the early *shabtis* seem merely to have applied this principle to the whole body. Certainly, they always bore the name of their dead owner.

At that time *shabtis* somehow became associated with servant-figure statues – little wooden models of servants to minister to the deceased; but as these gradually died out the *shabtis* began to lose their 'reserve body' status and themselves took on more and more of the servant-statue's function. By the Second Intermediate Period they had become little peg figures in tiny wood coffins with magic formulae written on them in black hieratic script. During the New Kingdom this '*shabti* formula' became standardized and almost invariable and made it clear that these servant statues, who now carried little hoes and adzes and other tools, were to sow seeds, breach dykes, water fields and shift sand for the dead person. On their left shoulder or across their backs they usually carry a seed bag, and their inscription always gives the names and titles of the deceased so there can be no mistake about whom they should serve. The '*shabti* formula' is in fact Chapter 6 of the *Book of the Dead* (see p. 88) and runs as follows:

> Glorifying the Osiris x, he or she says: O thou shabti, if the Osiris x is called upon, reckoned or accounted in the necropolis to do all the work which is done there, liability is removed from him there as an enforced labourer. If one is accounted at any time to sow the fields, to water the dykes, to row the sand from East to West or vice versa, 'I shall do it, behold me', you shall cry.

By the end of the New Kingdom the number of *shabtis* included in a burial had grown considerably. Not content with a handful of servants, some Egyptians took with them as many

Wooden shabti box with shabtis of the lady Henut-Mekhyt

as four hundred and one *shabtis*: one for each of the three
hundred and sixty-five days of their year plus thirty-six over-
seers. The overseer *shabtis* wore everyday dress according to
fashion and sometimes carried whips to make sure nobody sat
down on the job. Occasionally there were even scribe *shabtis*
so that the dead person would not have to do anything so
exhausting as his own account-keeping. By this time what had
started out as a custom for royalty had been adopted widely by
the Egyptian upper and middle classes. Pharaohs still used
shabtis, but on a grander scale. Royal *shabtis* are generally

69

Wooden model of breadmaking

larger and more splendid. They are often more numerous, too,
Seti I having had anything up to a thousand of them in his
tomb.

But by this time the ordinary *shabti* – generally made of
stone, wood, faience (glazed ware), pottery and occasionally
metal – had often become a pretty crude affair, mass-produced
with blank spaces for the owner's name and crammed into
large square *shabti* boxes with vaulted tops. Now that its
function had become so clearly defined and the idea of the
shabti so incorporated into funerary custom, the Egyptians
could afford to be a bit more slapdash in making it. There was
a final flowering of *shabtis* during the Saite Period (26th
Dynasty) but by the end of the Ptolemaic period *shabtis* died
out as rough bits of moulded faience, looking for all the world
like glazed jelly-babies. They had degenerated into mere
symbols of the old, carefully-executed servant statues. The only

thing which had not changed was the necessity for them to bear the owner's name. Without the name they were quite worthless.

While still under the general heading of *shabtis* mention should also be made of the wooden statuettes depicting the preparation of food and drink. Strictly speaking these are not really *shabtis* at all, but because they have a symbolic function rather like that of the *shabtis* they ought to be included.

Where supplying the dead person's diet was concerned the sickles, hoes and other tools included in the burial chamber were obviously of practical use. But until the end of the Middle Kingdom the Egyptians also used to make little wooden models of servants baking bread, butchering cattle, brewing beer and so on. By the New Kingdom these three-dimensional figures had been replaced by two-dimensional paintings on the tomb walls, and it was these pictured activities which kept the dead person supplied with food and drink. As long as there was a picture on the wall showing somebody brewing beer then the deceased was miraculously being kept supplied with beer.

Many Egyptians – Tutankhamun being merely one – were buried with a quantity of actual food and drink, enough to last the journey from life to after-life. There might be jars of wine, beer or water, trays holding little loaves of coarse bread, roast duck, dried fish, plates of figs and dates. Their tombs also

Left: Dish of preserved fish for consumption in the after-life. Right: Dish of figs for the same use

had special little offering-places in which the *ka*-priests charged with looking after them left regular offerings of food. What kind of food, how much food and for how long the supply was to be maintained were all clearly drawn up in the legal contracts with the mortuary priest which a rich person made before death.

As an additional guarantee that he would not starve, a dead person's relatives would often have several food amulets placed on his mummy. Among these might be amulets of trussed geese or oxen.

Osiris Beds

From the 18th Dynasty burial chambers often contained Osiris beds, which were boxes made of wood or pottery in the shape of the body of Osiris – represented as the mummy of a king. One was found, for example, in the tomb of Queen Tiye's parents, Yuya and Thuya. The frame of the one discovered in Tutankhamun's tomb was moulded in the shape of Osiris, hollowed out, filled with fertile Nile silt and planted with corn. Often, as in this case, the whole thing was then wrapped in linen so as to resemble a mummy. The sprouting green corn represented the resurrection of the earth every spring by reference to Osiris, whose own resurrection in turn symbolized that of the dead person.

This symbolism, like most metaphors, is best not pushed too far into literalness. The seeds would, of course, soon have sprouted underneath the bandages in the dark of the tomb; but unseen and untended their moisture would equally soon have dried up and they would have withered and died.

Osiris beds occurred frequently in New Kingdom burials; but since such burials are seldom discovered intact examples of such beds are quite rare.

We now move to the equipment the Egyptians used to safe-guard the body, whether in its actual (mummified) form or as they imagined it would be in the after-life. For a start, they could take certain steps physically to protect the mummy – such as enclosing it in an ever-growing nest of coffins.

Coffins and Sarcophagi

During the first two dynasties, coffins were made of plain wood (see p. 35). They were not in the familiar coffin-shape, how-ever, but were nearly square. The two longer sides were panelled, while the ends extended above the level of the coffin-lid, which was rounded. The body inside was folded into a crouch, knees drawn up under the chin, like a baby in the womb. It was held in this position by tight wrappings of gum-soaked bandages.

At this stage in history coffins generally went straight into the tomb as they were. It was only monarchs, or very high officials, who went to the trouble and expense of having sarco-phagi made in which to put their coffins. Queen Hetepheres of the 4th Dynasty (see pp. 140–3) had a very beautiful plain sarcophagus made from calcite, the translucent white Egyptian alabaster, whereas her son King Khufu (or Cheops) was buried inside a massive sarcophagus hewn from a huge block of granite. Not only was this the hardest material to work, it was also the most costly, since granite had to come all the way from Aswan in Upper Egypt. It is an indication of how seriously the Egyptians took the rites surrounding burial that they also used stone sarcophagi for their sacred animals (see p. 61). They frequently mummified animals, and the Apis bulls of Memphis (see pp. 61–2) are a good example of the length to which they would go. These bulls were as carefully embalmed as any king and then enclosed in granite sarcophagi sometimes weighing as much as 65 tons apiece. Even nowadays, to transport a block of stone weighing that much 450 miles down the Nile and then down into a catacomb at Memphis would pose an engineering

Outer and inner wooden coffins of the priest Hor

problem; but in an age which could rely only on wooden levers, sleds, ropes and sheer muscle power it must have represented an enormous expenditure of time and money and labour.

By the Middle Kingdom coffins had taken on their familiar rectangular shape, and usually had an inner coffin as well. They were decorated round the outside with a single horizontal line of inscription and on the inside with magic texts designed to help and protect the dead person in the after-life; occasionally there was even a map which would make it easier for him to find his way about in the underworld. On the outside of the coffin, opposite where the corpse's head would lie, were usually painted two *udjat* eyes (see under *Amulets*). They were always painted on the east side so that the deceased could look out towards the rising sun. Other essential decorative features on the outside of the coffin included an invocation to Osiris on the east side, the inscription running from north to south. On the west side of the coffin were prayers to Anubis and on the end boards prayers to Isis and Nephthys. The coffin-lids generally had a single row of hieroglyphs running from head to foot which was another prayer to Anubis (or sometimes to Osiris).

In the New Kingdom, coffins became mummy-shaped with a head and rounded shoulders. These first appeared in the 17th Dynasty at Thebes and were very large and heavily built in wood. Often they had a pattern of feathers incised or painted on them; the pattern was supposed to be protective and such coffins are known as *rishi* coffins after the Arabic word for feathers. Later, they were very beautifully painted with a representation of the dead person dressed in his best finery, a sort of full-length portrait, on the outside, of the person who lay within. Inside, like Chinese boxes or Russian dolls, were other coffins of decreasing size. The second was even more splendidly painted as an exact likeness of the dead person and was often topped off by a heavy wig fitted over the head; while the innermost coffin was practically moulded to the body itself, so closely did it fit. Occasionally it really was moulded to the body, being made of *cartonnage* – strips of linen soaked in plaster which then hardened exactly like the casts used today for setting broken limbs. Over this moulded face would be fitted a mask on which the most lifelike possible portrait would be painted, so that the mummy seemed almost like the dead person returned to life and merely asleep, wearing rings, kilt or gown, garlands of flowers and bead necklaces. The lower part of the mask covered the upper breast and was painted to imitate a broad, brightly-coloured bead collar.

The mask had a function of its own, too, which was to enable the *ba* (the soul which left the body by day to visit the outer world in any form it chose) to recognize its body when it came back at night. Ingenious as the *ba* was in assuming any shape, it was evidently quite unable to see through several layers of bandages and therefore needed help in finding its way back to the right mummy.

On early New Kingdom anthropoid coffins (18th and 19th Dynasties) the bands of inscriptions usually followed the principal external bandages of the mummy. Thus there is a single band from head to foot and then four horizontal bands, all coloured yellow. On the vertical band are the names and titles of the dead person and a prayer to Nut. On the horizontal bands are prayers to Thoth, Anubis, and the four Sons of Horus. In the panels thus formed between the bands are figures of these gods and *udjat* Eyes. The ground colour of such coffins is generally black, with a broad decorative collar around the coffin's 'neck'. The pectoral always had a picture of Re in his boat and there is usually a vulture, or Nut kneeling with outspread wings, painted below the forearms.

Between the 20th and 21st Dynasties the outsides of coffins were covered with figures in bright colours painted on a yellow ground. Sometimes the details of these figures were modelled in low relief. In addition to the large head-dresses and bead collars, a criss-cross of red and yellow braces was painted across the chest, and a pair of carved wooden hands was frequently added. On the lower half of the coffin there was a central god (or gods) with outstretched wings: the sun disc, a

Gilded plaster and linen mummy mask of a royal female

scarab (see section on *Amulets*), Nut, or a hawk, for example. Below and in the centre was a vertical band with prayers for funerary offerings to Osiris, Ptah-Sokaris-Osiris, Anubis and Re-Horakhty-Atum. The remainder of the lid was filled with figures worshipping these gods plus others such as Isis and Nephthys, and one or more of the following scenes might also have been shown:

1) the ram-headed sun-god in his boat,
2) the dead person adoring Hathor as a cow,

3) the dead person adoring Anubis and the four Sons of Horus,
4) the funeral and Opening of the Mouth ceremony,
5) the weighing of the heart,
6) Osiris enthroned,
7) the resurrection of Osiris,
8) the separation of Geb and Nut by Shu and
9) the demons of the underworld.

The interiors of such coffins were no less busy. Inside the rounded, head-shaped end was a human-headed *ba*-bird and on the floor of the coffin was a large central figure of Nut, Amenophis I, Osiris or a *djed*. The rest of the floor and the sides were decorated with scenes such as the Adoration of Re-Horakhty, Osiris or Anubis. In addition there would be rows of demons, while every free space was filled with sacred symbols like the *djed*, the *tit*, the *ankh* or the *udjat* (see the following section on amulets and scarabs for an explanation of these symbols).

Footboard of a wooden coffin showing the Apis bull carrying the mummy to the necropolis

Of the coffins dating from the 22nd to the 30th Dynasties, those between the 22nd and 26th are shallower and smaller, while those of the 26th to the 30th are disproportionately broad so that the faces are grotesquely large. These faces are painted red, yellow or green, and underneath them appear the usual broad collar and pectoral. There are no arms or hands. A single vertical column is inscribed with the funerary offerings text. Scenes commonly painted on the coffin include: the weighing of the heart, the *ba*-bird visiting the deceased, the dead person worshipping various gods, Thoth and Horus setting up the *djed*, and Anubis embalming the owner of the coffin. The texts chosen are most often chapters 89, 125 and 154 of the *Book of the Dead* (see below, p. 88). Inside, a painting on the floor of the coffin usually shows Nut or Sokaris standing.

From the 26th Dynasty to the Roman Period some coffins take on a rectangular form with a vaulted lid and protruding corner-posts, somewhat reminiscent of the early dynastic coffins. On the lid there might be the wooden figure of a hawk, and the whole of the outside is covered with pictures of gods or the dead person, plus the usual prayers for food offerings. In the Roman period itself the mummy lies in a cartonnage coffin, moulded to the shape of the dead person in everyday dress. A hollow plaster head might be placed over the real head, or over the face a wood panel, painted in encaustic with a portrait of the dead person (see the illustration of Artemidorus's coffin on p. 80).

As with coffins, the general shape of sarcophagi changed from rectangular in the Old and Middle Kingdoms to anthropoid in the New Kingdom.

Amulets and Scarabs

Once the mummy had been assured of physical protection by the embalming process and elaborate burial, the Egyptians felt they required the additional protection of magic to make quite sure. With the body, therefore, they buried various

Left: Mummy of indeterminate sex in rough anthropoid coffin
Right: Mummy case of Artemidorus, with a painted portrait panel

amulets or magic charms, each of which had a special significance and function all its own. These amulets might have been placed in the coffin or the funeral chamber, but were most frequently wrapped in while the mummy was being bandaged. X-rays of still-wrapped mummies invariably show different amulets scattered about the body, and because each had a specific purpose it usually appeared in a specific place. There were literally hundreds of different amulets from which the embalmers – acting on the request of the dead person's relatives – could choose, but the following is a short list of those which occur most often, including a handful which were considered essential.

(i) HAND AND FEET amulet. These had two functions. First, they could act as substitutes for the limbs they represented in case anything happened to them. In this way they fulfilled the same purpose as did the reserve heads mentioned earlier under *shabtis*. A foot amulet could in theory be a substitute for a foot and a leg as well, so the magic was clearly powerful enough to overlap a bit. Second, they could also restore to the dead person the powers associated with the hands and the feet, enabling him to be as skilful as ever and to get about with his old sprightliness. Similarly, face amulets could restore lost powers of seeing or talking.

(ii) The DJED PILLAR amulet, from the word *djed* meaning to be immovable. This conferred the power of stability and firmness. It was considered essential, and everyone was buried with a Djed Pillar. What it originally represented is not certain; but it is somehow connected with Osiris. It might be that god's stylized backbone and ribs, or again it might be the trunk of a tree with its branches lopped off (in one version of the Osiris myth his coffin floated to Byblos in Phoenicia, where it lodged in the branches of a young tamarisk tree which lifted it ever higher off the ground as it grew). The appropriate spell in the *Book of the Dead*, chapter 155, reads:

> Raise thyself, Osiris. You have your backbone (again), thou still heart! Raise thyself upon thy

Funerary amulets and equipment. Left to right: Combined ankh, djed and was made from glazed composition; glazed composition winged scarab; glass heart amulet; plaster-stiffened linen hypocephalus showing the four Sons of Horus before a cow goddess; glazed composition plaque showing Anubis and winged udjat; carnelian girdle of Isis tit amulet; glazed composition udjat-eye; glazed composition four Sons of Horus; glazed composition papyrus sceptre; carnelian leg with foot amulet; glazed composition hand amulet

side. . . . I have brought to thee the djed of gold in which thy heart rejoices. To be said over a djed of gold suspended by a fibre of sycamore . . . As for the one on whose neck this amulet is placed, he shall be among the excellent spirits in the necropolis on the first day of the year, like those who are followers of Osiris.

The amulet was worn on the chest.

(iii) The ANKH amulet represents the straps of the Egyptian sandal. It conferred on the wearer powers associated with life and living.

(iv) The UDJAT EYE of Horus, or the Hawk's Eye amulet, from the Egyptian word *udjat* meaning whole or sound, a reference to the restoration by Thoth of the eye which Horus lost in one of his struggles with Set while trying to succeed to his father's (Osiris's) throne. This was beyond question the most powerful amulet they possessed, and gave the wearer health. The right and left eyes represented the sun and moon respectively. This amulet could sometimes also stand as an offering of food.

(v) The TIT amulet or the so-called Girdle of Isis. Usually made of a red material signifying the blood of Isis, the TIT protected and conferred strength. It was worn on the chest.

(vi) The HEART amulet or the IB. The Egyptians believed that the heart rather than the brain was the seat of intelligence. This amulet ensured that the wearer went forth in the after-life with all his wits about him. It was used at all periods of Egyptian history and was mostly placed on the mummy's chest. Depending on the kind of stone from which it was carved it had a slightly different function, as the *Book of the Dead* makes clear:

Gold amulets of Mut, Thoth, Amun and Ptah

Chapter 26: (On lapis lazuli) 'Whereby the heart is given to a person in the underworld.'

Chapter 27: (On green felspar) 'Whereby the heart of a person is not taken from him in the underworld.'

Chapter 29b: 'Another chapter of the heart upon carnelian. I am the Heron, the Soul of Re, who conducts the glorious ones to the Duat. It is granted to their *bas* to come forth upon the earth, to do whatsoever their *kas* willeth. It is granted to the *ba* of the Osiris x to come forth upon the earth, to do whatsoever his *ka* willeth.'

(vii) GOD amulets. These were a whole series of amulets devoted to about fifty principal deities. They conferred the characteristics associated with the gods according to myth and legend. The most common were:

a) ISIS amulets and NEPHTHYS amulets. Isis and Nephthys were sisters, and gave overall protection to the dead.

b) MIN amulets looked after one's fertility or virility.

c) THE FOUR SONS OF HORUS. Horus was a falcon god who became identified with the son of Isis and Osiris. His own sons appear as amulets in sets of four; they collectively stand for the protection of the dead. In this form they are most familiar on the stoppers of canopic jars (see p. 89). The four sons were:

Hapy (who had a baboon's head)

Imsety (who was human-headed)

Qebhsenuef (hawk-headed)

Duamutef (whose head was that of either a jackal or a dog, nobody is quite sure which).

d) ANUBIS amulets were named after another jackal-headed god (there was more than one) who was the god of embalming as well. These amulets were also for the protection of the dead, but like many of the generally protective amulets, were often worn by the living as well.

(viii) Scarabs are amulets in the shape of the Egyptian dung-beetle (Latin name: *Scarabaeus sacer*). The dung-beetle lays its eggs in little bits of dung which it then rolls with its legs into perfect spheres. To the Egyptians, the sight of a newly-hatched beetle emerging from a ball of dung looked like magic – a kind of spontaneous generation. The beetles thus acquired mystical significance and another Egyptian god was born: *Kheper* (the word was their name for the beetle), who symbolized the rising sun, which similarly appeared to be re-born each day after being rolled around the heavens and disappearing at night. Thus *kheper* or scarab amulets guaranteed the wearer new life and resurrection. They were extremely important and survive in vast numbers.

(ix) HEART SCARABS are much larger than ordinary scarab amulets and were only worn by the dead. There was never more than one on a body, but its

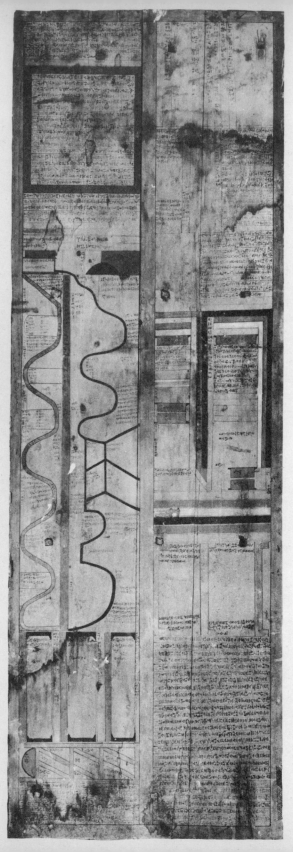

Floor of the outer wooden coffin of Gua, which shows a map of the underworld with two paths leading to it

presence was essential. It was invariably made of black or green material and was hung round the neck so as to rest over the heart. On its flat underside was an inscription, the so-called 'heart formula' from Chapter 30b of the *Book of the Dead*.

This spell was connected with the Egyptians' belief that the dead person had to be justified or found worthy before he could be guaranteed resurrection. In essence this myth was not unlike the later Christian one of a Day of Judgement. In the Egyptian version the dead person's heart was weighed in a balance against a feather which represented Truth (cf. also the story of Belshazzar's feast in Daniel 5:27: 'Thou art weighed in the balances, and art found wanting.'). Anubis stood and watched the scales, Thoth (the ibis-headed god) kept the record, and an extremely sinister-looking monster made up of the nastier parts of crocodiles, hippopotamuses and jackals lurked in the background to snap up the heart if it failed the test. The 'heart formula' was simply a spell telling the heart to keep quiet and say nothing in case it weighed the balance down against its owner with a guilty confession.

There is a heart scarab in the British Museum, made of green jasper and with a human face instead of a beetle's head. It is set in a gold rectangular base on which is a roughly-chased hieroglyphic inscription of an early form of the 'heart formula'. It was made for King Sobkemsaf, a 17th Dynasty king (c. 1640 B.C.) and disappeared from his tomb in one of the great tomb robberies during the reign of Ramesses XI nearly six hundred years later. By sheer chance we know the names of the actual robbers concerned from a papyrus that gives an account of their trial (for the full story see ch. 5).

When the leader of the gang, a stonemason named Amen-pa-nefer, confessed: 'We collected the gold we found on the noble mummy of this god, together with his amulets and jewels which were on his neck and the coffins in which he was resting' he was referring to this particular heart scarab. What happened to it during the next three thousand years will probably never be known; but in 1835 it came into the BM's collection via an antiquities collector named Athanasi. According to the sale catalogue 'This unique and very curious relic was taken from the breast of a male mummy found at Thebes'. It is in the Museum to this day for all to see – the very scarab referred to in that insignificant trial of more than three thousand years ago.

The Book of the Dead

The *Book of the Dead* is not really a book at all, but a collection of ancient spells. By convention, each spell is called a 'chapter', since the Egyptians themselves knew the collection as the *Chapters of Coming-forth by Day*.

The spells were copied out on papyrus and either pushed into the coffin with the dead person or placed in a separate wooden box which was topped by a curious statue, the Ptah-Sokaris-Osiris figure. There were probably about two hundred spells in all, but there is no copy with all two hundred in existence. What happened was that the person made his own selection of chapters before he died, or else his family later paid a scribe who would then copy out as much as he had been paid to. During the 18th Dynasty, though, the pool from which the selection of appropriate texts might be made had become more or less standardized.

The spells were nearly always copied in cursive hieroglyphs (not in hieratic, see p. 212) and written with a brush on papyrus. They were generally illustrated with miniatures done in ink or paint and are often very beautiful. They enabled the dead person to assume an identity which would help him to take the powers of various gods, to arrive safely in the Fields of the Blessed and to leave his tomb when he felt inclined.

Canopic Jars and Canopic Chests

These were the containers into which a corpse's entrails were put during the mummification process. They were then placed in the tomb with the mummy. They started in the Old Kingdom as boxes with compartments inside. Queen Hetepheres' embalmed entrails were discovered in just such a box – in her case it was a very beautiful alabaster chest – individually

Glazed composition plaque of the goddess Nephthys and the top half of a glazed composition figurine of Isis suckling Horus

Reserve head of an official, made from limestone

wrapped and still soaking in a dilute solution of natron. This practice was reflected in Middle Kingdom Canopics which often consisted of a wooden chest compartmented into four, and in each compartment – and hiding the linen parcel of insides – was a cartonnage mask a few inches high in the same style as the mummy's mask.

At all periods from the Middle Kingdom onwards the entrails were put in jars which fitted into the compartments of the chests. Ideally, the jars were made of stone, but they were often of glazed ware, pottery or even wood.

The stoppers of the jars originally represented the four Sons of Horus (see p. 85) but were human-headed. Hapy looked after the lungs;Imsety guarded the liver; Qebhsenuef watched over the intestines and Duamutef protected the stomach.

After the 18th Dynasty, however, the stoppers took on the Sons' animal heads, only Imsety remaining human-headed. Then in the 21st Dynasty (1085–945 B.C.), and in that single dynasty only, the Egyptians suddenly changed their embalming custom for some reason known only to themselves. They stopped putting the viscera into Canopic jars; instead, they went back to embalming and wrapping them separately in linen, but then replaced them inside the body cavity. Each bundle had tied to it a little wax figure of the appropriate Son of Horus. Yet even this sudden change of practice betrays the Egyptians' extraordinary conservatism in never discarding old customs, since they continued to include perfectly redundant canopic jars in these burials although they were sometimes only dummies made with solid bodies, a custom which became almost universal in the Ptolemaic period.

It is partly this conservatism which makes the tangle of Egyptian religion, mythology and ritual so complicated. They tended to hang on to their old beliefs and habits even when these had been overtaken by new ones: they simply incorporated the old system into the new. Over some three thousand years of dynastic history their mass of magic, ritual, spells, customs, beliefs, dogmas, habits and fashions merely went on getting bigger. It is remarkable that anyone in the later dynasties should ever have managed to decide exactly what was the right way of doing anything.

Soul-houses

The Middle Kingdom tombs of less rich people tended not to have sets of models showing various activities (bread-making,

Pottery model soul-house with two storeys

Wooden model of a funeral barge, showing the mummy on a bier

brewing etc.). Instead they took with them model houses made of pottery, in the forecourts of which offerings were represented. The soul-house was intended to provide food and a house for the *ka*.

Hypocephali

These are discs like small dinner plates mostly made of cartonnage. They were placed under the heads of Saite Period mummies (26th Dynasty) and were painted with extracts from Chapter 162 of the *Book of the Dead*, a spell which would keep the mummy warm.

Model Boats

Model boats appear quite frequently in Middle and New Kingdom tombs. Their purpose was to ferry the dead person up and down the Nile on Osirian pilgrimages to Abydos and Busiris.

4

FUNERALS AND TOMBS

Practically all we know about the Egyptians' burial customs comes from the pictures on their tomb walls or from the little illustrations in papyri. These are fairly common, but even so the meanings of many details are still obscure. (This is also true of the vignettes illustrating embalming, which equally contain mythological allusions which we simply cannot understand.)

Their pictures of funerals appear to be concerned first and foremost with transporting the sarcophagus or coffin from the house or mortuary to the tomb. This nearly always involves crossing the Nile before reaching, by long and difficult paths, the necropolis in the desert or mountain valley. Such a thing would obviously have been necessary if the dead person had lived on the side of the river opposite to that of the cemetery, as at Thebes. But it is quite likely that this representation dates from the days when the body of the pharaoh was towed in a funeral barge to Busiris in the Nile Delta and then down to Abydos for the Osiris festivals. The notion of such a royal pilgrimage had gradually been adopted by everyone as a symbol of what a proper funeral entailed, even though in reality it meant something as simple as crossing from one bank of the river to the other.

A typical middle- or upper-class funeral procession would have left the dead person's house early in the morning and made its way slowly down to the Nile. It would have been noticeable from a fair distance on account of the professional mourners wailing and groaning. These were men and women hired for the occasion and wearing the blueish-grey colour of mourning. Their job was to smear their faces with dust and mud, tear their clothes, beat their heads and pull their hair out while weeping loudly in case the procession seemed a bit thin or suspiciously unmoved. They helped each other along as if blinded by tears and grief somewhere near the sarcophagus which was being towed on a sled near the end of the procession.

At the head of the cortège came servants carrying bunches of flowers and trays of cakes, bread, duck, haunches of beef and vegetables; and behind them more servants bearing jars of water and wine, bottles of oils and pots of unguents. These would be followed by men with boxes on their heads which contained the dead person's provisions, a little ahead of those with the *shabti* boxes and ritual equipment. Next would come a group carrying furniture: folding chairs, armchairs, stools, beds, even dismantled chariots, in addition to chests of clothing and linen. A groom might come next, perhaps, leading a favourite horse. The group behind him would have the vases for offering libations, the Canopic chest, the Canopic jars, the dead man's swords, bows and arrows, military batons (if he was a military man), necklaces and pectorals. The kind of personal possessions would obviously have depended on the dead man's profession. A scribe, for example, would have palettes and drawing and writing implements.

At this point the mourners came, followed closely by a mysterious object called a *tekenu*. It looked like a bundle trussed roughly into the shape of a human torso and onto which a head had been fixed, although sometimes the head was left off. Usually it was covered in the skin of some animal and was dragged on a sled towards the cemetery. Somewhere near the cemetery it was 'sacrificed' with the oxen which had pulled the sled and, originally, with some Nubian prisoners as well. After the beginning of the Dynastic Period the prisoners were merely sacrificed symbolically; no doubt this represented a harking-back to the pre-dynastic days when there had been human

Ani's funeral (above) and the Opening of the Mouth ceremony (below).

sacrifices, days which lingered on into the 1st Dynasty in the form of servant-burials around the earliest mastabas at Abydos, when servants were buried with their dead master so as to be able to continue their service in the after-life.

This *tekenu* rite clearly dated back a long way, the animal skin representing the manner in which bodies were wrapped in the old predynastic sand-burials. The *tekenu* had a function exactly akin to that of the 'scapegoat' (cf. Leviticus 16:10) by which a mock animal was charged with all the shortcomings

From the Book of the Dead of Ani

and impurities of the dead person in order to be sacrificed in his stead at the end of the funeral ceremony.

After the *tekenu* a statue of the deceased might have been dragged along on another sled. It was accorded great prominence: incense was waved before it throughout the journey as it bumped and jolted its way up the stony track. Behind it and in front of the coffin walked the *sem*-priest who was the priest in charge of the whole burial service. He would have worn his traditional costume of a panther skin which would certainly

97

have distinguished him from the other priests: the *ka*-priests, the *hery-heb* priest who recited 'glorifications' and the *wt*-priest who had been in charge of the embalming.

The coffin itself was placed in a boat which was mounted on a heavy wooden sled pulled by oxen and yet more servants. The sides of the boat were covered with decorated wooden panels although they were sometimes simply draped with rich embroideries. (One of these coverings was found in the Deir el Bahri cache; it had belonged to a certain Isemkheb and was made of soft leather worked with brightly-coloured figures and hieroglyphs so that it looked like mosaic-work.) There would quite likely have been two women with the coffin itself, kneeling on the sled at either end. They were called *kites* and played the parts of Isis and Nephthys. Behind the coffin came the family and friends and, if the deceased had been an important person, all sorts of officials and bigwigs, some of whom would be carrying offerings and gifts of their own. If the dead person had been an important man his harem would probably have been represented by several distraught ladies whose grief must have been considerably intensified by bleak thoughts of their own future.

No doubt this colourful and noisy procession would have drawn curious onlookers, barking dogs and infants rendered silent by the noise and spectacle as it made its way towards the river bank. There would have been many who looked enviously at the signs of wealth going past them; many more who could gauge at a single knowing glance how much the man had been worth; and the very poorest of all might not even have known enough to be envious, such was the gulf between rich and poor.

At the river the procession would be met by half a dozen boats which – like the mourners – had been rented for the occasion from some sort of funeral agency. The party would come to a ragged halt by the jetty and gradually divide itself among the various boats. The mourners' boat had a large cabin whose sides were hung with brightly-decorated cloth or leather, whereas the 'hearse boat' had a shrine-shaped cabin adorned

Left: Tomb painting showing the crossing of the Nile and the Opening of the Mouth ceremony. From the tomb of Menna at Thebes. Right: Bringing the mummy to the tomb. Tomb of Amenemint, Thebes

with bouquets of flowers and palm branches. The heavy coffin was reverently eased on board and into the cabin, followed by the female members of the family, while the *sem*-priest waved his censer and filled the boat with fragrant wafts of smoke. Meanwhile, the professional mourners had been handed up onto the roof of their boat, which was to tow the 'hearse boat' across the river. They faced backwards, addressing their continuous wailing towards where the coffin lay, occasionally breaking into a unison dirge.

> Pull hard to the West, the land of truth. The women of the Byblos boat [merely the name for a kind of passenger ship] are weeping, weeping. In peace, in peace to the West, O Praised One, come in peace. Would that this day might become eternity for me, as we behold you intent upon it [i.e. eternity], as you go to the land (where) men are changed.
>
> (This particular chant was taken from Tomb no. 49 at Thebes, that of Neferhotep who was Chief Scribe of Amun at the very end of the 18th Dynasty, probably under Ay.)

99

Mummy on a bier, flanked by Isis and Nephthys. From the catacombs at Alexandria

Four more craft waited to take the rest of the procession: all the servants with their burdens, the furniture, and those of the friends of the family who wished to attend the burial service itself. After a certain amount of waiting and manoeuvering they would cast off, the oars would dig into the brownish current and the little fleet would head slowly out across the river towards the barren escarpment on the other side, now beginning to shimmer with heat haze as the sun climbed in the sky. The drawings and illustrations of the river crossing in the tombs and papyri often make the occasion look very stately: colourful and crowded, perhaps, but frozen into silence by the stylized and emblematic treatment – caused, no doubt, by the implicit recognition that the archetype of this journey was that of the pharaoh himself. Below this surface, though, the participants were no doubt experiencing rather timeless emotions: some grieving loudly, some shocked and silent, some pleasantly melancholy, some rather drunk but not showing it, some whose new sandals were killing them and who watched glumly the approaching hills which would shortly have to be climbed.

Others, like the captains and crews of the barges, were merely doing a job of work which they hoped would go off without a hitch because there was another funeral to do that afternoon. As they neared the landing-stage a crowd would have mustered to greet the party. Probably there would have been a handful of opportunists with their stalls selling bunches of flowers for those whose floral tributes had already wilted, or religious knick-knacks for those who felt rather too conspicu-ously empty-handed. Gradually they would all disembark, shuffling down the gangplanks onto the dock and re-forming into a procession once more. Then the servants would shoulder their master's possessions, the oxen take up the strain on the ropes hitched to the coffin sled with a creak of wood, the mourners wail (not, perhaps, very loudly at this point since like the boat crews they had another funeral to do and anyway they were saving their breath for the climb), and off they would all set again.

Soon the stony path had skirted the last of the irrigated fields on the river bank and began to climb the mountain. One or two of the limping or elderly relatives might now and again shoot a covert glance back over their shoulders at the growing panorama behind them. In the bright heat they could see across the river to the opposite landing stage and, behind it, the shimmering town they had left. At the dock on the far side they could make out the six funeral ships, now returned and making ready for the next procession.

Meanwhile the cortège was nearing the necropolis. The party had been joined by *muu*-dancers who were capering about at the front, and snatches of thoughtful music drifted back to the plodding relatives as musicians at the entrance to the cemetery came out to greet the party. Eventually they all came to a halt by the tomb, which had already been prepared. But before the dead man could be buried, there was a vital last ceremony to be performed by the *sem*-priest. This was the so-called 'Opening of the Mouth', which hopefully would restore

to the mummy all the faculties which physical death and embalming had temporarily removed.

The *sem*-priest, still in his panther skin, celebrated this ritual
by simultaneously representing Horus (Osiris' son) and also
the dead person's own son. The mummy was unloaded and
stood upright on a little patch of sand at the mouth of the tomb.
With various prayers and incantations the *sem*-priest touched
the mummy's face twice with an adze and once with a flint
instrument with a forked end and then did the same to the
ka-statue. The dead man could now see, hear, speak, eat and
move his limbs. One of the oxen was coaxed forward and, with
much noise and mess and men straining to hold it down, was
slaughtered and its right foreleg sawn off. The right foreleg
was believed to contain the ox's physical powers, and it was
promptly presented to the mummy's mouth. The ox was a
symbol of virility, so possibly the haunch was thought to
restore sexual potency to the mummy.

Throughout these activities the mourners had kept up their
lamentations: the *hery-heb* priest recited his 'glorifications' and
the rest of the *ka*-priests scurried about performing minor
rituals with anointing-vases full of holy oil, blowing puffs of
incense-smoke about and pouring libations of milk or water on
the ground at various points. What with the dead ox, the
sobbing relatives, the loud incantations and the gentleman in
the panther skin it was quite a carry-on, and as far removed as
could be imagined from the bleak and stoic graveside ritual of
a 20th century Christian burial. As the ceremonies reached
their climax the grieving widow could be heard, her voice
raised piteously above the clamour, addressing her dead
husband:

'I am your wife Meryt-Re. O Great One do not abandon
me (for) your counsel is good, O good father! See, while I am
far away you do it like ... (?) ... while I go alone with the
singers. See, I am behind you; but you, the one who loved
to speak with me, are silent.'

And the women echo her cries:

> 'Praise! Praise! Safe! Safe! Safe! Safe! Wail untiringly! O
> the misfortune! The Good Shepherd goes to the land of
> eternity. The multitude of mankind is taken from you; you
> are in the land which loves solitude. He who loved to move
> freely [lit. 'open his legs in walking'] is enclosed, bound,
> walled-in. He who was rich in fine linen is sleeping in the
> linen of yesterday.'

This last mention of linen was probably a reference to the fact
that the bandages in which the dead person was wrapped were
often household linen showing clear signs of wear. The linen
was sometimes marked with the name of the owner but this
name was not always that of the deceased.

Somewhere amid all this was a rite referred to in papyri as
'the breaking of the red vases'; but since it is never fully explained it remains obscure, although it presumably had some
powerful symbolic significance. Meanwhile, the mummy was
replaced in its nest of coffins which were then carried into the
tomb and lowered down the shaft into the burial-chamber. If
the sarcophagus were one of those enormously heavy stone
boxes it would have been prepared in the chamber and the
mummy in its nest of coffins lowered down to it. This was the
burial itself; and once the lid of the sarcophagus or outer coffin
had been eased shut all the furniture, clothing, provisions, goods
and chattels were handed down from above ground and stacked
around the chamber. Close to the sarcophagus would be
placed the Canopic chest with its four jars, and also the boxes
of *shabtis* – all things which the dead man would need most
urgently. One or two of the grave-goods would be ritually
broken, thus 'murdering' them so that their doubles could
accompany the dead person.

Finally, when the last object had been stacked into the now
full chamber, the priests offered up a final prayer, the relatives
took their leave and everybody climbed mournfully back out
of the lamplit gloom into the blazing heat of an Egyptian mid-

day. Men began throwing rocks and stones down the shaft of the burial chamber, sealing it off with rubble. Once the shaft was full a mason came with mortar and laid some stones to block the mouth, walling up the mummy's 'House of Eternity' and like as not finishing off with a layer of plaster into which he pressed the oval necropolis seals.

While this was going on the servants had produced a funeral feast which they had somehow brought along with all the other provisions. The feast was usually held round the doorway of the tomb itself, or somewhere nearby in the necropolis where there was a convenient patch of shade. The mourners, who would already have shaken some of the dust from their hair, straightened their dishevelled blue robes and dried their *kohl*-streaked eyes, tucked in, no doubt glancing at the sun to estimate how soon they could decently leave so as to arrive back in town for their next engagement. As they ate and drank a harpist would probably have lingered among the pillars and porticoes nearby, singing improvised songs in praise of the dead man or well-worn favourites about the shortness of life and the general lot of man:

> 'Bodies pass away since the time of the god and young men come in their place. Re shows himself at dawn, Atum goes to rest in the Western mountain; men beget, women conceive. Every nose breathes the air. Dawn comes, their children are all gone to their tombs.'

This was taken from Tomb no. 50 at Thebes, which happened to belong to someone called Neferhotep – this time a Divine Father of Amen-Re in the time of Horemheb, some years after Ay.

This, then, was the sort of funeral a reasonably wealthy New Kingdom Egyptian could have expected. The averagely poor peasant would obviously not have been sent off in such style, and would probably just have been carried wrapped up in a shroud or in a crude wooden coffin on the shoulders of his family to the paupers' cemetery, which was often in the middle of the necropolis and surrounded by the laboriously-prepared tombs of the rich. For the poor there were yawning trenches always ready. Their rites were hurried; and at evening a thin layer of sand was spread over the day's burials. Sometimes people were buried simultaneously in batches of twos and threes. Some of the bodies were bandaged in coarse linen, others were crammed into palm-frond baskets. No funerary furniture accompanied such people to the grave: only the tools of their trade, their sandals and some cheap amulets and jewellery. One Theban Poor-Pit was unearthed in which sixty layers of bodies were discovered without the bottom layer having been reached.

A pharaoh's funeral, on the other hand, would have exceeded that of a wealthy man by a similar degree. The principal ceremonies might have been the same, but they would have been far more elaborate, infinitely longer and performed by armies of priests. It was, after all, a State occasion; and just as the treasures buried with the king were more numerous and altogether fabulous, so the ritual was suited to the passing (and renaissance) of a god.

There was another quasi-'State' occasion called the Beautiful Festival of the West Valley. This was a public holiday held between the harvest and the inundation in the second month of summer. In it Amun left Karnak and crossed the Nile to visit the mortuary temples of his illustrious descendants, and especially that at Deir el Bahri. The Festival went on for at least a fortnight. Commoners used it as an excuse to visit their own family dead, holding picnics at the tombs and taking offerings and bouquets of flowers to the chapels while accompanied by singing and dancing.

The Tomb

Throughout most of their long history the Egyptians buried their dead underground. This method of disposing of their bodies was also aimed at preserving them and is a true reflection of their preoccupation with physical, and not just spiritual,

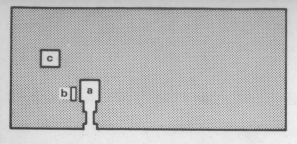

a chapel at south-east corner
b serdab
c shaft to mummy chamber

Groundplan of an Old Kingdom private mastaba

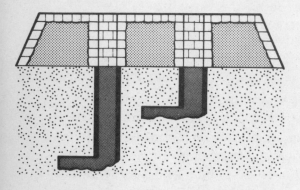

Section of a mastaba with two burial shafts

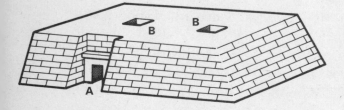

Mastaba with entrance to chapel **A**
and shaft openings in roof **B**

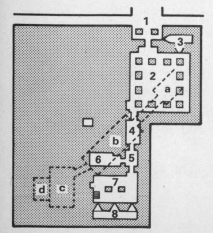

Groundplan of the mastaba of Ti at Saqqara, Fifth Dynasty

1. Vestibule
2. Colonnaded court
3. Serdab
4. Corridor
5. Second corridor
6. Side chamber
7. Tomb chapel
8. Serdab

a steps to underground passage
b underground passage
c vestibule
d Tomb chamber

Private Old Kingdom Mastabas

immortality. Plenty of other cultures have adopted quite different ways with their dead, believing that a corpse is no more than a potential health hazard. The Parsis of India, for example, have their *dakhmas* or Towers of Silence, which are round brick or stone buildings where the naked corpses are laid out to be picked clean by vultures, a process which generally takes less than an hour.

This would have been quite unthinkable to an Egyptian, to whom preservation of the body was of paramount importance. Their tombs were designed for strength and durability although the style and shape varied from period to period. A brief summary follows.

Mastabas

The early pre-dynastic sand-burials such as 'Ginger's' (see pp. 33-4) were nothing more than shallow graves covered with a heap of sand and rocks. The rocks were partly to stop jackals from digging up the body and partly to mark the grave for relatives who would wish to visit it from time to time with fresh food and drink. Once Egypt had been united under a central administration, and a clearly-defined class of officials and wealthy property-owners had emerged, a mere heap of rock was no longer a suitable way of marking an important person's grave. The custom began of building a low superstructure over the grave made of dried mud bricks. It was either solid brick right through or had a central core of rubble with a brick skin round the outside. Its shape was rectangular, with walls sloping inwards to a flat roof. In fact, it was modelled on the dead person's house if he were a commoner or on the royal palace if he were a king. One of the 1st Dynasty mastabas at Saqqara, which has been dated to the reign of Anedjib, contains within its superstructure a kind of stepped pyramid which was probably a survival of the old Upper Egyptian style of tomb. Thus two kinds of tomb are combined into one. Quite possibly this stepped mound was the forerunner of the step pyramid proper.

The mastaba developed in flat Delta-type country rather than in hilly or mountainous regions since on a more or less featureless landscape it would show up well. These structures reminded more modern Egyptians of the benches they sat on to drink coffee and chat, so they called them *mastabas* after the Arabic word for bench.

Mastabas of the first three dynasties had walls of the kind known as 'palace façade': a sort of corrugated effect with alternately recessed and 'proud' courses of bricks arranged vertically like a series of narrow squared columns. Some mastabas had this stepped panelling on the east face only, and during this period the panelling eventually became simplified into two niches on the east face: one at the north and the other, slightly larger, at the south end. In front of this south-eastern niche was a small open-air enclosure which became a little chapel whose inner face contained a false door. By the end of the period the chapel had been moved into the main body of the mastaba itself. There was usually a shaft leading from the

Mastaba field at Saqqara

roof at the north end down to the one or more chambers carved out of the rock deep below ground. The passageways leading to the actual burial chamber were often blocked with stone portcullises as a safeguard against intruders. It was in this kind of early mastaba that the Egyptians' unembalmed bodies began to decay, leading them to adopt mummification.

From the 4th Dynasty onwards mastabas were made entirely of stone instead of mud-bricks. The chapels were still there, either outside or inside the main building at the south-east corner, their interiors decorated with brightly-coloured bas-reliefs cut into the walls. The offering-place in the chapel consisted of a false door through which the dead person's spirit was supposed to pass in order to help itself to the food and drink laid out on the offering-table. The false door effectively separated the world of the living from the world of the dead.

The main shaft of the mastaba now led down from the middle of the roof, and at the bottom was a short passage leading to a rectangular burial-chamber lined with limestone. Since by now embalming was in full swing there was a niche in the pavement wall to hold the mummy's canopics. Underground, these mastabas were fairly stark and simple; but above ground they were becoming ever more grand. Now they not only looked like houses from the outside but were becoming more like them inside as well. If the dead person were still to go on living in the after-life, as if death had been no more than a temporary inconvenience, with all his earthly possessions around him and waited on hand and foot by his servants, carved in relief, or as wooden models or later as *shabtis* – then he would need his tomb to be as much as possible like the house he had left. Indeed, some 2nd Dynasty mastabas at Saqqara even had imitation bathrooms and latrines along with their bedrooms, living-rooms and harems. The rock-cut underground part of the mastaba of Ruaben at Saqqara has its funerary chamber at the end of a long corridor with side rooms leading off, and in front of it is a dummy apartment with latrines.

The chapel which had once been outside had receded further

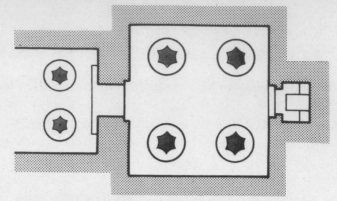

Plan of a Middle Kingdom rock-cut chapel at Beni Hassan

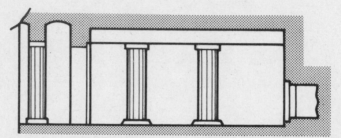

Section of a rock-cut tomb chapel at Beni Hassan

Facade of a rock-cut tomb chapel at Beni Hassan

Plan of Middle Kingdom non-royal rock-cut tomb chapel

and further into the mastaba's superstructure, and had finally developed into a number of rooms whose walls were decorated with splendid painted bas-reliefs depicting scenes of everyday life. Giving on to the offering-place in the chapel was the *serdab*, a tiny walled-off room connected with the world of the living only by a slit at eye-level. Inside the *serdab* was the dead person's *ka*-statue, and the odour of the food and drink offered in the adjoining chapel was expected to waft to it through the slit, although, as we shall see in Chapter 6, it was the 'spirit' of the food which passed in to the *ka*-statue.

Rock-cut Tombs

As mentioned earlier, mastabas were built from scratch on open ground. They were generally set at regular intervals around the unfinished tombs of reigning kings in 'streets' so that when the pharaoh died the important dead would be

Rock-cut Old Kingdom tomb at Giza with two-pillared porch

lying in orderly rows close by him. Another and quite distinct type of tomb also developed in the Old Kingdom but is essentially typical of the Middle and New Kingdoms. This was the rock-cut tomb which, as the name implies, was excavated from cliffs and hence only appears in hilly regions such as on the West bank of the Nile at Thebes or Aswan. One or more rooms were carved out of the cliff to form the chapel, sometimes with a forecourt in front, and usually from the floor of the main room (or from a special shaft room) a shaft or passage led down to the burial chamber. Sometimes the main room was pillared and had a pillared porch before it; certainly its walls were always covered in incised or painted decorations. There was usually a secondary chamber or recess behind it for statues. The earliest rock-cut tombs are the 4th Dynasty ones at Giza, some of which have a sloped façade to imitate the sloped sides of the mastaba.

Pyramids

But by far the most impressive, as well as the most celebrated, Egyptian tomb-style was the pyramid. The pyramid itself really started in the 3rd Dynasty when the pharaoh, Djoser, decided he wanted his mastaba to be 'everlasting'. His architect was Imhotep, a man whose genius and fame were so great that he practically achieved the status of a god in succeeding generations. Imhotep had Djoser's tomb stoutly constructed of stone, thus making it the first large stone-built monument in Egypt's history. He enlarged the usual mastaba shape until it was very big and square, then built five more square mastabas of decreasing size on top of the first. The result was a flat-topped pyramid in six steps.

The curious thing is that Imhotep himself probably did not think of his design as a new entity in itself, but rather as a huge confection of six mastabas; either that or the design exemplified the innate conservatism of the ancient Egyptian mind. For entrance to the burial chamber and corridors was still via the usual mastaba shaft, although of course this was now buried under a heap of five other mastabas. Imhotep therefore cut a horizontal tunnel leading from the top of the shaft to the outside, a piece of design which was later to be found in proper cased pyramids, which sometimes have their entrances well above ground-level.

In any case, the size and elegance of Imhotep's creation must have impressed all who saw it, and it started a fashion. Djoser's successor, Sekhemkhat, began another like it but left it unfinished; and Sekhemkhat's own successor probably began one but left that unfinished as well. Then the last king of the 3rd Dynasty, Huni, started a tomb at Meidum which, had it survived, would have been the first true pyramid, since it was built in steps but its faces were cased flat with stone. Like the others, it too was left unfinished and had to be completed by the first king of the 4th Dynasty, Sneferu. Sneferu was obviously much taken by pyramids for he built two of his own. The first, at North Dahshur, is a true pyramid but it is bent: the sides do not form a continuous slope of the same angle. He followed this at South Dahshur with the first true surviving pyramid.

From Huni's Meidum pyramid onwards, pyramids were never again built on the 'pile of mastabas' or step system. They were all conceived from the outset as complete in themselves. They were built of rubble-and-rough-block core faced with the finest quality limestone from the Tura quarries. It is this casing which later generations stole, block by block, for other buildings, which is why the Giza group look so tatty and unfinished. It is therefore quite wrong to refer to the 'steps' of the Great Pyramid at Giza as some writers do; the 'steps' are not the walls of mastabas but simply the courses of stone without their limestone casing.

The true pyramid was so impressively large and strong that beside it an ordinary mastaba looked like the heap of mud it mostly was. It became the prerogative of the pharaoh to build himself a pyramid; and since in any case nobody else could possibly have afforded the prodigious cost, pyramids were exclusively royal. The pyramid's solid geometrical shape, jutting up out of the flat northern country, looked truly immovable and, with its glassy sides of dressed stone on which not even time could get much grip, everlasting.

The adoption of the smooth-sided pyramid is also thought to be connected in some way with the cult of the sun whose centre was at Heliopolis. The cult was becoming very powerful and influential at this point in the Old Kingdom. The centre-piece of its worship was a conical or pyramid-shaped stone called a *benben*, whose very tip caught the first rays of the rising sun at dawn. The *benben* was set on top of a stone pillar and – as may easily be visualized – this pillar with its pyramidal top later developed into the obelisk. When a pyramid was built there would always be a small flat area left at the very top since the last course of stone would probably be a single cube. To form a point and complete the pyramid a capstone or *pyramidion* would be placed on top. It is possible that there was a degree of

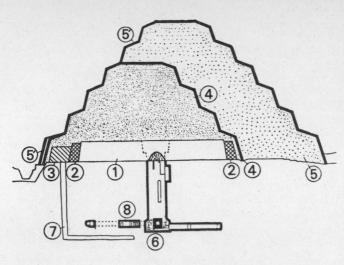

1. square mastaba with core of local stone faced with Tura limestone

2. extension of 14 feet

3. extension of 28 feet to the east side

4. extension of 9 feet 6 inches on each side and mortuary temple begun on north side

5. extension towards the north and west

5'. facing of dressed Tura limestone

6. shaft and burial chamber

7. 11 vertical shafts with corridors leading westward from them

8. rooms containing panels of blue-glazed tiles

Plan of the Step pyramid

Step pyramid of Djoser at Saqqara with the chapels of the Heb Sed Court in the foreground

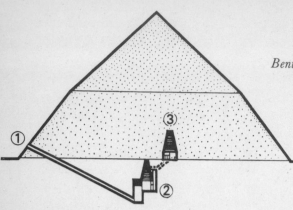

1. entrance
2. lower chamber with corbelled roc
3. upper chamber with cedarwood framework beneath the floor

Pyramid of Meidum looking west

1. first ascertainable form of the superstructure, a seven-stepped pyramid
2. enlargement to an eight-stepped pyramid
3. extension to a geometrically true pyramid
4. entrance to the pyramid
5. burial chamber

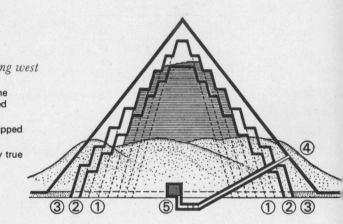

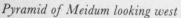

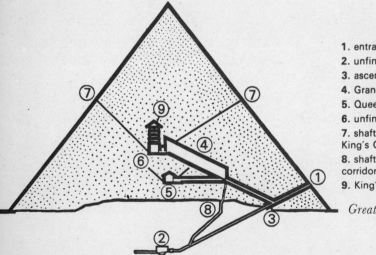

1. entrance to descending corridor
2. unfinished chamber
3. ascending corridor
4. Grand Gallery
5. Queen's Chamber
6. unfinished shafts
7. shafts leading to surface from King's Chamber
8. shaft leading to descending corridor
9. King's Chamber

Great pyramid looking west

association between the *benben* and the *pyramidion* which saw the latter as completing at one and the same time an elegant geometrical solid and a spectacularly high object of religious awe.

The Egyptians gave the pyramid the name of *mr*, meaning 'the place of ascent'. Seen as a staircase to the heavens this was in line with the cult of the sun, and it could also have referred to the pharaoh's resurrection. On the other hand, if the *benben* were thought of as representing the sun itself then the straight edges of the pyramid might have represented the sun's descending rays. Either way, the ultimate shape of the pyramid and its Egyptian name probably have close connections with the sun cult. Plenty of more fanciful – not to say completely dotty – theories have been put forward to explain the genesis of the pyramid, and these are dealt with in the final chapter.

The pyramid's entrance was usually in its north face, possibly because of some significant connection with the Pole Star. From it a passageway led to the burial chamber which was either just inside the main body of the pyramid or, more often, carved out of the rock beneath it. Sometimes, though, a pyramid would be built around a natural outcrop of rock (like the Great Pyramid), which meant slightly less construction work besides guaranteeing complete solidity. In this case some of the chambers and passageways inside would be hewn out of the rock and it would be unnecessary to go much below ground level, if at all.

The equivalent of the mastaba's chapel was the pyramid temple which stood separate from the pyramid itself in front of the east side. It contained several rooms, usually undecorated before the 5th Dynasty, in which daily offerings were made. Some of the rooms were for members of the public who might come to worship the dead king, whereas others were reserved for his priests alone. From this temple led a covered stone causeway, its walls often finely decorated, which ran down to the Valley Temple built either on the river bank or at the point where cultivation ended. This other temple was used only for embalming and ritual purposes, and its main function after the

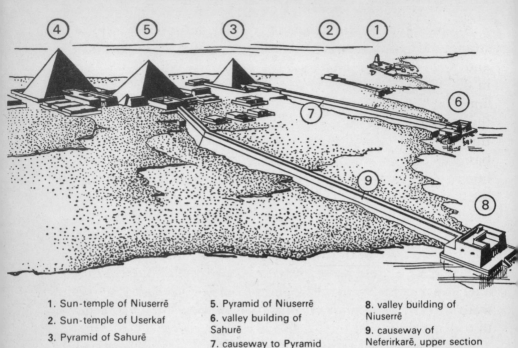

1. Sun-temple of Niuserrē
2. Sun-temple of Userkaf
3. Pyramid of Sahurē
4. Pyramid of Neferirkarē

5. Pyramid of Niuserrē
6. valley building of Sahurē
7. causeway to Pyramid of Sahurē

8. valley building of Niuserrē
9. causeway of Neferirkarē, upper section rebuilt for Niuserrē

Fifth Dynasty pyramids at Abusir – reconstruction to show a pyramid complex

funeral was more as a magnificent entrance to the causeway leading up to the pyramid itself.

These three, then, are the main types of Egyptian tomb, ignoring the early sand-graves: mastaba, rock-cut and pyramid. All three persisted more or less simultaneously and more or less throughout Egyptian history. The reason for this was at least partly due to the local burial customs dictated by the terrain. And although the pyramid had begun as a royal tomb and went on being used as such until the 18th Dynasty (and still later by the Kushite kings) it, like much else of Old Kingdom royal custom, had long since been adapted by commoners. It was all part of the apparent 'democratizing' process which became possible after the radical upsets of the First Intermediate Period had lessened for ever the godlike status of the pharaoh.

A fourth kind of tomb became popular, however, but it is a strange hybrid which is a mixture of mastaba, rock-cut tomb and pyramid. It was developed in the early Middle Kingdom in the cliffs of the West Bank opposite Thebes by the Inyotef family whose political power in southern Egypt for a while threatened the pharaoh in the north until they finally overthrew him and ruled Egypt themselves. Their tombs were basically of the same design as a typical upper-class Egyptian's home. There was a short ramp up to an open courtyard cut in the hard soil. In the side walls of this courtyard were doors leading to the tombs of their retainers, while the rear of the courtyard was also pierced by doorways giving the appearance of a colonnade of pillars; hence such tombs are called *saff* tombs, from the Arabic word for 'row'. This row of doors opened into a lengthy hall running parallel to the front. From the opposite wall of this hall led one or two rooms, the innermost with access to the burial chamber.

But the *pièce de résistance* of these tombs was a small pyramid

The three pyramids of Giza

Middle Kingdom saff tombs at Thebes

made of bricks and usually put up behind the courtyard, high on the cliff above the tomb. It was generally painted white to look like limestone, and a sort of miniature *benben* was cemented on top. On each of this little *pyramidion*'s four faces – at least, during the New Kingdom – was carved a picture of the dead person worshipping the sun god.

In addition to these *saff* tombs there were also the private tombs of the Middle Kingdom, which at Thebes were not greatly different from the *saff* tombs of royalty but which, away from Thebes, were rock-cut tombs with pillared porch and main hall now at right angles to the façade and running far into the mountain. On open terrain, though, private individuals still went on using the mastaba.

During the New Kingdom at Thebes private tombs had rock-cut chapels of T-shaped plan above a burial chamber reached from a courtyard. A broad hall running parallel with the façade formed the cross-bar of the T, its walls covered with scenes of everyday life. A long inner room, set at right angles, with a statue niche at its end and funerary scenes on its walls,

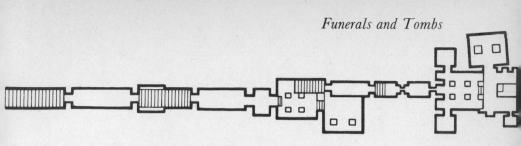

Plan of the tomb of Seti I in the Valley of the Kings

formed the upright of the T. It was now that the pyramid – long out of use as a royal tomb – was successfully 'tamed' by commoners. Many of these Theban tomb-chapels were capped by a sharply-pointed brick pyramid, but it is an architectural form associated especially with the tomb-chapels of the workmen of Deir el Medina which, during the Ramesside Period (19th–20th Dynasties), consisted of a court, enclosed on three sides by a wall, from which a staircase or shaft led to underground

Valley of the Kings, Thebes. Foreground: Tomb of Tutankhamun. Behind right: Tomb of Ramesses VI

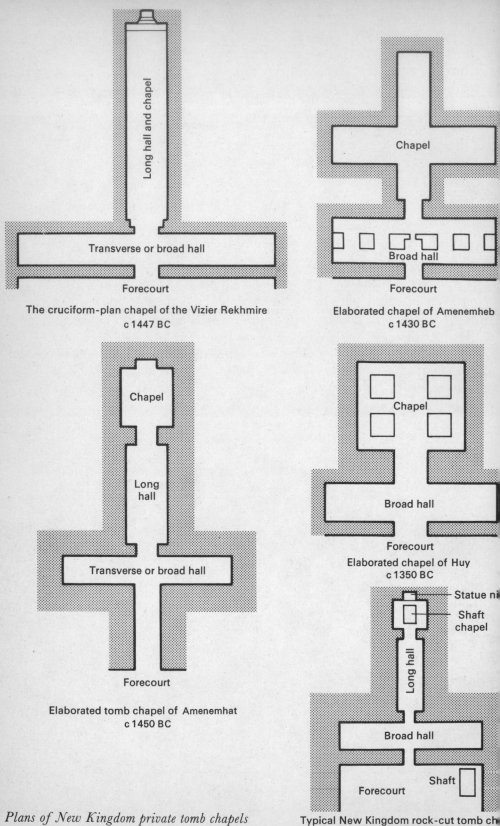

Long hall and chapel

Transverse or broad hall

Forecourt

The cruciform-plan chapel of the Vizier Rekhmire
c 1447 BC

Chapel

Broad hall

Forecourt

Elaborated chapel of Amenemheb
c 1430 BC

Chapel

Long hall

Transverse or broad hall

Forecourt

Elaborated tomb chapel of Amenemhat
c 1450 BC

Chapel

Broad hall

Forecourt

Elaborated chapel of Huy
c 1350 BC

Statue ni

Shaft chapel

Long hall

Broad hall

Forecourt

Shaft

Plans of New Kingdom private tomb chapels

Typical New Kingdom rock-cut tomb ch

burial chambers with vaulted ceilings. A chapel on the fourth
side of the court, often with a pillared porch, consisted of a
single room with vaulted ceiling decorated with painted scenes
and with a *stela*, a tablet of stone bearing inscription, recessed
in the rear wall. Such funerary *stelae* often have two hawks'
eyes on top through which the dead person might see the light
of day, and an inscription which would perpetuate offerings if
real ones failed to materialize. This so-called *hotep di nesu*
formula began: 'A gift which the king gives' and always included the wish for 'thousand of bread and beer, oxen and fowl,
alabaster [vessels] and clothing'. ('Thousand' simply meant
massive quantities.)

Outside, mounted on the chapel roof, was a hollow brick
pyramid capped with a limestone *pyramidion*, with its sides
picturing the deceased worshipping the sun god. A niche in the
face of the pyramid overlooking the courtyard held a statuette
of the dead person, sometimes shown kneeling and holding a
tiny *stela*. Such was the trivialized end of the grandest of
Egypt's monuments.

Left: A reconstruction of private tombs at Deir el Medina with pyramidions
Right: Pyramid-shaped brick chapel roof at Deir el Medina

This is by no means a complete survey of ancient Egyptian tombs, but the basic design of the three main tomb styles remained more or less unchanged, while details became modified according to fashion and place. The role played by the terrain was all-important since it dictated the style of the tomb. To sum up with a series of generalizations:

(i) Mastabas are found only in flat areas (usually in the north), but they were used throughout the Dynastic Period, first by royalty as well as commoners but later only by commoners.

(ii) Pyramids are always royal. In the Old Kingdom they are all sited in northern Egypt since this was where the country was ruled from. In the Middle Kingdom they are found further south but, like mastabas, pyramids are always sited on open ground. Pyramids died out in Egypt after the 2nd Intermediate Period although a few were built later in the Sudan.

(iii) Certain rock-cut tombs at Thebes in the New Kingdom took over the elements of the Middle Kingdom *saff* tombs with their *pyramidions* for commoners. Royalty using rock-cut tombs were buried in underground chambers (*hypogea*) at the end of a succession of corridors, pillared halls and staircases. Rock-cut tombs were in use throughout the Dynastic Period, although, for obvious reasons, only in hilly regions.

Some of the changes in the above tomb-styles were dictated by increasing attentions of professional tomb-robbers (see next chapter). In the case of pyramids the entrance was moved and concealed some distance away from the pyramid itself and the Middle Kingdom pyramids incorporated blind alleys and an elaborate 'doubling back' system inside which had been invented during the reign of the 12th Dynasty king Sesostris II.

Such protective systems were also adopted by contemporary mastabas, and the rock-cut tombs in the Valley of the Kings likewise had their temples moved far away to the edge of the cultivation lest their position should betray that of the actual tomb. When the entrances of these rock-cut tombs were blocked up with rocks and shale after the burial they must very soon have become undetectable. This could explain how

Tutankhamun's modest tomb was completely forgotten when, some generations later, the Egyptians began excavating a rather grander burial place for Ramesses VI only a few feet away – something they would never have done had they known how close the older tomb was.

Pyramid Texts and Funerary Books

A vital part of any tomb was the collection of texts and spells either brought in with the dead person (as with the *Book of the Dead* papyri which were usually wrapped with the mummy) or carved, inscribed or painted outside or inside the tomb. To remind ourselves briefly of the theology:

The death suffered by Osiris was the common lot of all mortals. But as Osiris rose again, so could a man if the same magic formulae as had been originally spoken by Isis were pronounced for him by a faithful son. He would then go to Osiris, be united with him and become one with him. Admission to the realm of Osiris depended on three things: the correct incantations and the recitation of magic formulae; the weighing of his heart by Thoth; and a trial undergone before Osiris and forty-two judges to prove that he had led a virtuous earthly life and was free from mortal sin.

Like the *Book of the Dead*, the various other funerary books and texts were not so much like books as loose collections of spells which could be drawn upon for an appropriate selection. The choice of book and its doctrine depended very much on the period, theories about the underworld and the relative importance of Re and Osiris varying in accordance with the funerary beliefs of the time. Thus the early Pyramid Texts (from the 5th Dynasty onwards) are concerned with the pharaoh's journey to the circumpolar stars or the Fields of Iaru – the heavenly fields where ploughing and reaping were done as on earth (plenty of *shabtis* needed!). Another doctrine placed the dead in Duat, the underworld, which was divided into twelve regions corresponding to the twelve hours of night.

There is some mention of Osiris in these texts, but mostly they concern a solar destiny, since Osiris had by then not yet reached his great Middle Kingdom popularity. The spells in the Pyramid Texts were simply a collection of utterances to help the king reach heaven. Many of them were the prototypes of certain spells in the *Book of the Dead*, and some of them were already immensely old and dated back to long before the building of the pyramids. One of them speaks of the dead person removing a brick from his tomb, another of throwing the desert sand from his face – clear references to early mastaba and desert burial.

Between the 6th and 12th Dynasties (i.e. during most of the 1st Intermediate Period) Coffin Texts appeared which were devoted almost exclusively to magic formulae which would enable the dead to see daylight again. Thus the sun god dominates the texts, the wish being that as he conquered the dark so might the dead person conquer the other world. This could only be achieved by magic: none had an automatic right to the light. Magic had to be used to open the portals of the horizon and cross the celestial regions. The Coffin Texts expressed all the usual wishes that the dead person might enjoy earthly pleasures such as food, drink, sex and pure air. Bodily completeness, freedom of movement and the ability to transform oneself were all very important since the other world was full of enemies such as serpents and monsters.

In some 11th Dynasty coffins from el Bersheh there were maps of the other world, since the accompanying texts were so difficult and obscure that the only hope of the dead person's orientating himself on arrival was with the aid of a map. In this other world the dead encountered two twisting paths separated by a lake of fire. The earth-path led to Rostjau and the water-path led to the lake of Rostjau. The entrance to the first was guarded by a gate of fire, while the entrance to the second was kept by a ram-headed crocodile with a knife. The text was called the *Book of the Two Ways*, and the spells useful in overcoming these disconcerting phenomena had a decidedly Osirian flavour. The *Book of the Two Ways* thus marks the transition from the Pyramid Texts and Coffin Texts on the one hand to the New Kingdom funerary books on the other.

By the New Kingdom a compromise had been reached between the solar and Osirian doctrines. Osiris had his kingdom in the underworld, and the sun god visited it every night in his boat, bringing light to the dead as he traversed the kingdom. Three new sets of texts appeared: the *Book of That Which Is In The Underworld (Imy Duat)*, the *Book of Gates* and the *Book of the Night*. All three are really just a development of the *Book of Two Ways*. By this period we find the underworld described in some detail. Its twelve regions are called caves or fields and are arranged like the Egyptian nomes (the provinces into which Egypt was administratively divided). Each has a god at its head, ruling from a capital city peopled by all sorts of gods, genies and dead spirits. The ram-headed sun in his boat navigates the Underworld Nile which flows through each region in turn. Like the earthly Nile, it has sandbanks to impede the sun's progress, and the dead have to help tow his boat when it runs aground. Occasionally their help is not enough and the sun has to change his boat into a serpent or use some of Isis's magic.

The idea that the underworld was full of enemies must have persisted, since the sun's boat was in these texts assailed by evil genies. In the territory of the 7th Hour a huge serpent named Apophis attacks. The sun god makes a crafty detour to avoid him but Apophis nearly foils him by drinking the river dry. From then on it is more or less plain sailing, although this eventful journey must have been a wearisome one to make every other twelve hours, even for a god.

In the Late Period some of the main pyramid texts turned up again. The New Kingdom funerary books meanwhile persisted and were joined by some new ones, including the *Lamentations of Isis and Nephthys*, the *Book of Apophis*, the *Book of Breathings* and the hopefully-named *Book of May My Name Flourish*. These were mainly written on a roll of papyrus and put into the coffin.

Tomb Scenes

The paintings inside tombs are often the only source of detailed information we have about everyday life in Egypt. As with everything else, the type of decoration varied according to period.

The chamber walls of Old Kingdom mastabas were lined with fine quality limestone which was incised and then painted. These reliefs were raised, of the type called bas-relief. The reverse, the shallow-cut *reliefs-en-creux*, in which the designs are sunk below the surface of the stone, are usually only found outside where the sunlight can make the shadowed effect stand out. In the New Kingdom the poorer quality of the limestone (for example, that at Thebes) meant that it was only possible to have carved decorations if the walls were first lined with top-quality stone. Instead of this expensive process the Egyptians adopted the reasonable alternative of plastering the walls and then painting them with water colours although the occasional tomb – like that of Ramose – did have incised scenes. Before the Ramesside period, the painted background to most New Kingdom tomb decorations was a pale grey-blue, perhaps a reminder of the colour of mourning. From the Ramesside period onwards the Egyptians favoured a yellow background so that their tomb scenes – mostly religious – look like vignettes on a vast unrolled papyrus. The ceilings of these New Kingdom tombs were brightly painted in extremely intricate patterns, as if in imitation of highly-decorated textiles.

The subjects of these tomb scenes also varied from period to period. For example, they became more or less profane during the 18th Dynasty, being mostly concerned with everyday life and the dead person's own earthly career. After the end of that Dynasty's Amarna period, however, there was both popular and 'State' reaction against the heresies of Akhenaten (see Chapter 6), and the pictures became more exclusively religious as the cult of Amun was re-asserted.

Counting geese. From the tomb of Nebamun at Thebes

Some of our best insights into the daily life and funerary beliefs of Egypt come from these tomb scenes. Often they depicted people at work of various kinds, frequently watched by the noble whose tomb it was and who had employed them when he was alive. The snatches of conversation recorded above the figures in the pictures might have been said by ordinary people in practically any country and at practically any time. Written in colloquial Egyptian, they provide a welcome relief from the heavy formality of the hieroglyphic funerary texts.

Some examples may be taken at random. From the 5th Dynasty mastaba of Ti, above a scene of catching birds in a clap-net:

'There's a catch of birds for your arms, sailor, if you keep quiet.'

Or, above a sailing scene in the same tomb:

'Watch the rope. The wind's freshening behind you.'

From another Old Kingdom tomb, above a picture of butchers at work:

'Take his two horns; turn his head well back so that we can butcher him. Fix your cord. Hurry, friend.'

In the Old Kingdom mastaba of Ptahhotep and Mera there is an illustration of boys exercising.

'Your arm's much stronger than his. Don't be gentle with him,' is written over it with a sort of jovial brutality which, combined with a suitably feudal obsequiousness, characterizes many of the illustrations in the tomb of an 18th Dynasty noble named Paheri at el Kab. In front of some men ploughing is written:

'Hurry, leader, forward with the oxen. See the prince is standing watching!'

Above a couple of men breaking up clods of earth is the exchange:

'Get a move on, mate; let's get it over with,' to which the self-righteous reply is: 'I'll do more than what I owe the noble, so shut your mouth.'

The same servility is apparent in a snatch of conversation between an overseer and some men carrying basketsful of corn on a pole.

'Hurry it up there,' commands the overseer, 'the water's coming' (a reference to the annual flooding of the Nile) 'and it'll reach the baskets.' To which a man with an empty basket says: 'Doesn't this pole spend all day firmly on my shoulder? But that's how I like it.'

Above some women are gleaning:

'Give me a hand. Look, we'll come back in the evening; don't let's have any of yesterday's ill-feeling, you can stop it today.'

And a man carrying flax charmingly replies to an old peasant combing flax:

'Quick, stop nattering, you bald old fellow of a labourer!'

Contracts for Eternity

Finally, some mention should be made of the way in which upper-class Egyptians tried to ensure that their tombs would be looked after 'for eternity' as they hoped. They fully realized that it was all very well having an immensely lavish burial and leaving behind dozens of lamenting relatives and servants all pledged to keep them supplied with provisions and prayers. They knew that time passes, and pledges lose their solemnity and finally are forgotten altogether. And what happened when those who knew you and served you died themselves? How could you be certain that your descendants in a hundred years' time would be remotely interested in going up to your chapel every so often with food?

The king had his own funerary priests, his *ka*-priests, from quite early on. They lived near the royal tomb on land he had bequeathed them and with the revenue from that land. In return, their job was simply to minister to the *ka*-statue, perform rituals, make offerings and generally be responsible for the upkeep of the tomb. From the king's point of view, at least, it was quite an ingenious arrangement since he had left the priests their land only on condition that they fulfilled their duties. If they failed, the king could rely on some future generation to cut off their funds, sack them and appoint someone in their place. At the very least this shows how sophisticated the Egyptian legal and bureaucratic system had become. It was all down in black and white in the form of a series of contracts, so it was no longer a matter of someone making well-intentioned promises on behalf of his own descendants: the undertaking was legally binding.

Good examples of such contracts tying the funerary priests to the service of the dead person are the ten made by a 12th Dynasty nobleman named Hepdjefau. By these contracts the dead Hepdjefau in the person of his *ka* arranged for daily offerings to be made to a local god and in return had daily offerings set before himself. The contracts (example overleaf)

131

THIRD CONTRACT

TITLE

Contract which the Count, the Superior of Priests Hepdjefau, justified, made with the official body of the temple, to wit:

What Hepdjefau receives

There shall be given to him bread and beer in the first month of the first season, on the eighteenth day of the Wag-feast. [A festival of Osiris and the dead celebrated on the 18th day of the first month of the Egyptian year.] List of what shall be given:

Register of names	Jars of beer	Flat loaves	White loaves
Supervisor of priests	4	400	10
Announcer [herald]	2	200	5
Master of secrets [sacristan]	2	200	5
Keeper of the wardrobe	2	200	5
Overseer of the storehouse	2	200	5
Keeper of the wide hall	2	200	5
Overseer of the house [i.e. chapel] of the *ka*	2	200	5
Scribe of the temple	2	200	5
Scribe of the altar	2	200	5
Lector priest	2	200	5

What he pays

He hath given to them for it 22 temple-days, from his property of his paternal estate, but not from the property of the count's estate: 4 days to the Supervisor of priests, and 2 days to each one among them.

Definition of 'Temple-Day'

Lo, he hath said to them: 'Behold, as for a temple-day, it is 1/360 of a year. When ye therefore divide everything that comes into this temple, consisting of bread, of beer, and of meat for each day, that which makes 1/360 of the bread, of the beer, and of everything which comes into this temple, is the unit in these temple-days which I have given to you. Behold, it is my property of my paternal estate, but it is not the property of the Count's estate; for I am a priest's son, like each one of you. Behold, these days shall belong to every future official staff of the temple, since they deliver to me this bread and beer, which they give to me.'

Conclusion

Lo, they were satisfied with it.

also outlined special arrangements for festivals. The dead person's participation in making divine offerings and enjoying them was all-important; but in case of some unforeseen catastrophe or failure such offerings were also depicted on the walls of his tomb and pictures of food and drink incised on his own offering-tables. He also wrote up an invitation to casual passers-by to say a shortened version of the *hotep di nesu* offerings formula.

As one reads Hepdjefau's contracts and wonders how long they were effective, one is struck once again by the extraordinary confidence the Egyptians felt in the unchangingness of things. They seemed never to have doubted that their system would last 'for ever', and they thought, built and wrote accordingly. And yet the contracts are perhaps too detailed, too much the product of an obsession with trying to cover all the angles and every possible contingency. Perhaps the very attempt to lay a legal obligation on unknown people still to be born is at some level an admission of failure: that a law cannot restore a memory or bring back to life somebody long dead. By accident, it turns out that Hepdjefau's name lives on, although the civilization he relied on to sustain his *ka* has vanished.

5

TOMB ROBBERS

So much concern with the power and the glory of ancient Egypt and the fabulous riches with which the pharaohs were buried makes it easy to overlook an important fact: that the ordinary Egyptian was slavishly poor. Only the royal family, the nobles, priests and local land-owners had any wealth at all; the vast majority of the population were working people who owned practically nothing. Thousands must have lived their lives without ever seeing anyone else much better off than themselves, and a man would have counted himself rich if he could die leaving his son a donkey and perhaps a thin gold ring.

Yet an Egyptian living near a royal capital or a royal graveyard would have seen – and perhaps joined in – one of the vast funeral processions of an important official. He would have watched in awe as the pick of the person's belongings were carried into the tomb: gold and silver ornaments, rich clothes, exquisite furniture, even chariots. If the dead person was a member of the Royal Household, or even the pharaoh himself, then there would have been many times more treasures and of such value as to be practically meaningless to a watching peasant. He would have been dazzled and terrified by the display of sheer power passing by him which so demonstrated the huge gulf between the near-gods who ruled him and his own insignificance. He would have given it scant thought, though; there was nothing to think about it – it was simply how things were. He expected his rulers to be buried in the same style as he had expected them to live.

Green jasper heart scarab in a gold setting. From the tomb of King Sobkemsaf

No doubt there was a popular saying in Egypt then as there is in most countries now to the effect that 'You can't take it with you when you go'. But the Egyptian aristocracy believed that they could; so they did, and in as much quantity as they could manage. They vanished into the earth with their treasures, but they marked their resting-places by gigantic monuments. Early in the Old Kingdom when the great pyramids were built the pharaohs lay near the Nile beneath thousands of tons of beautifully-constructed stonework up to 481 feet high. The pyramids rise up from the desert, clearly visible for miles around, and to the more thoughtful peasants they must have seemed like glaringly obvious 'X marks the spot' clues to buried treasure.

It is clear that some of the braver of these poor Egyptians were willing to have a go at stealing it. They would have to have been brave, partly because of the penalties if they were caught, but also because of the divine aura which surrounded the pharaohs even when dead. The ordinary punishments would have been bad enough, no doubt, since the Egyptian legal system could pass sentences such as sending people into exile in the desert with their hands or noses cut off. Grand theft of the King's possessions would no doubt nearly head the list of the worst crimes an Egyptian could commit, so any thief who was caught could probably have expected to be impaled on a stake or to suffer some other equally unpleasant death.

But an illiterate Egyptian would have feared more than mere

physical punishment. In Old Kingdom times he would have been brought up from childhood to think of the pharaoh as a god on earth, so powerful that it was dangerous even to touch him in case the contact killed you by a sort of divine electrocution. The idea of breaking into a pharaoh's tomb where his mummy lay inhabited by his spirit would surely have been frightening enough, even to a fairly unimaginative person, but he knew that the king was additionally protected by all sorts of minor gods and demons.

Yet despite all this, tomb-robbing flourished and it was necessary to appoint official guards to the Royal graveyards such as the 'necropolis police' at Thebes. As an additional safeguard the architects who designed the tombs and pyramids, once they had realized that mere size was no real protection, installed complicated devices such as trick passageways which came to a dead end, and huge stone portcullises which would swing down and seal entrances. The physical dangers of tomb-robbing became considerable, since in a structure the size of the Great Pyramid it might be necessary, once one had managed to get inside, to dig a tunnel hundreds of feet long towards where one thought the king and his treasure lay. There was no guarantee that one wouldn't miss the burial chamber altogether after months of intense effort. It was also possible laboriously to remove (or tunnel round) plug after plug of stone blocking a passageway before coming to a dead end and discovering that it was a blind alley deliberately meant to mislead. Many a hastily shored-up tunnel roof must have collapsed on the robbers, no doubt trapping some of them until they died of thirst or injuries and the scorpions scuttled in from the desert to investigate their bodies. As will be seen later, the same traditions of robbery survive today, and the risks run are exactly the same as ever they were. During an excavation at Giza in 1969 archaeologists came across the emaciated body of a man lying beside a partly opened sarcophagus, his hand still stretched out to reach inside it. In his coat pocket was a newspaper dated 1944, doubtless the year in which he died.

When the Egyptian pharaohs did their utmost to prevent robbers from breaking into their tombs it was not simply the thefts which they feared. These were bad enough of course, because they believed they would need their treasures and possessions in the after-life. But they also knew that any robber with strong enough nerves to break past spells and barriers into the last resting-place of a god would not be very scrupulous when he got to the body. Everyone knew of the gold rings and amulets set with precious materials beneath the bandages of the mummy, and since a robber in a hurry would not be too careful, the body itself might be badly damaged, particularly if it were already old and fragile.

The tombs were therefore guarded by professional guards; but not surprisingly these necropolis police themselves turned out to be less than reliable. It must have been a boring job at the best of times, patrolling a remote cemetery, throwing stones at the occasional passing jackal, watching over people who had died perhaps hundreds of years before but whose tombs had been rashly guaranteed careful protection 'for ever'. Plenty of other jobs would have seemed far more attractive – joining the army and seeing the world, for instance, or even being a simple farmer down in the lush green fields on the banks of the Nile. These were just the sort of attractions that a royal scribe named Amenhotep had in mind when he composed a curse which, he hoped, would convince the guardians of his own tomb that any slackening-off of zeal on their part would lead to a horrid fate. Indeed, the curse extended to anybody who might even cause the guards to neglect their duties. If the guards allowed the tomb to fall into decay, or if anybody else tried to lure them away with offers of a better job, then they knew what to expect. They had been warned:

> [Amun's] uraeus shall vomit flame onto their heads, destroy their flesh and eat up their bodies .. Their boats shall capsize in the sea and they shall be swallowed up . . . Their sons shall not succeed them. Their wives shall be raped before their very eyes. They shall be doomed to the knife on the day of

Agricultural activities in the Field of Reeds.
From the Book of the Dead of Anhai

the massacre . . . Their bodies shall waste away because they shall go hungry and be without food, and their bodies shall die.'

Despite such threats, the mortuary guards were capable of more than simple dereliction of duty, as we shall see later. First, we should mention a couple of curious incidents relating to tomb-robbing in the Old Kingdom. The first concerns the 1st Dynasty King Djer. When Sir Flinders Petrie was excavating his tomb at Abydos late last century he found a skeleton arm wearing four beautiful bracelets. The arm had been pushed

into a crack in the wall of the tomb, and ever since then Egyptologists have been trying to work out whose arm it was and how it got there. One possible explanation is that at some time in the distant past some robbers broke into King Djer's tomb but were disturbed or actually caught red-handed. Perhaps one of them had just time enough to stuff the arm (which he had presumably torn off in trying to remove the bracelets) into the crack in the wall, intending to come back later to retrieve it. It is also possible that this might have been done by one of the local excavators working for Petrie while the tomb was being cleared. Either way, we shall probably never know. As for whose arm it was, it is assumed that it belonged to a woman and that therefore the most likely explanation is that it came from the body of one of Djer's wives who would at that time have been buried in the same tomb as the king himself.

About four hundred and fifty years after King Djer died something happened which has left another unsolved mystery. It concerns Queen Hetepheres, who was the wife of King

The weighing of the heart before the twelve great gods. From the Book of the Dead of Ani

Sneferu, who in turn was the founder of the 4th Dynasty and the man who built the first-ever true pyramid. Queen Hetepheres' son was Khufu, the pharaoh whom the Greeks later knew as Cheops. (It was Cheops who built the most famous of all pyramids, the Great Pyramid of Giza, at a time when pharaohs were at their most god-like and Egypt at the peak of its power as the dominant nation of the Near East.)

According to the custom of the time, Hetepheres would have been buried beside her husband's tomb at Dahshur. Imagine the surprise of archaeologists, then, who in 1925 were digging a good forty miles away at Giza and came upon what seemed to be Queen Hetepheres' burial. The entrance of the shaft leading to the burial chamber was camouflaged under a pavement on which the smaller pyramids of Khufu's three queens stood, so it was clear that the tomb had been built at least before Khufu's first wife had died. Hetepheres' tomb turned out to be a room hewn out of rock at the bottom of a shaft nearly ninety feet deep which was filled with stone blocks. But odder still, the archaeologists who first broke into that chamber which had laid undisturbed for more than 4,000 years found a complete mess. Instead of the orderly arrangement of treasures which would befit a royal burial, there was a litter of decayed wood and collapsed furniture lying higgledy piggledy about the floor.

Inscriptions on metal strips inlaid in the wooden objects said that they belonged to Queen Hetepheres, and indeed all her toilet things, her razors and tweezers, were there, pushed at random into the boxes together with chips of stone as if they had been hurriedly scraped up off the floor in handfuls.

This was very strange. Flashing their torches round the chamber, the excavators thought at first that this burial chamber, like so many others, had been robbed. But then they caught sight of the Queen's sarcophagus – a great stone coffin so large that it could only have been lowered down the shaft on end. There was also the sealed Canopic chest bearing her name and still containing traces of ancient sludge. But when they opened the sarcophagus – with extreme difficulty, owing to the weight of the stone lid – they found it empty. The Queen had gone.

Where was Queen Hetepheres and what had happened to her? We can only guess the answer, but one theory seems most likely. Shortly after Hetepheres died – probably less than ten years after her son Khufu came to the throne – her tomb near to Sneferu's at Dahshur was broken into and robbed. During the course of the robbery her body was destroyed (tomb-robbers sometimes set fire to the mummies they unearthed, perhaps to render them harmless and incapable of revenge, an interesting parallel to the later European idea of burning witches or of burning vampires as the only way of annihilating them other than driving a stake into their hearts. The mummies would have burned well owing to all the oils and unguents used in the embalming process.) The priests and mortuary guards responsible for the safety of her tomb must have been appalled when they discovered what had happened. It was out of the question that they could go to the pharaoh and announce that his mother's tomb had been raided and her body stolen.

So they decided on a daring and risky plan. They probably told Khufu that there were signs that his mother's tomb had been tampered with, but owing to their own enormous efficiency and dedication to their duty, they had managed to catch the intruders and nothing had been touched. At which point Khufu might have told them that for safety's sake they had better transfer the burial to Giza where his own tomb, the Great Pyramid, was being constructed. It was of course essential that Khufu should not ask to see his mother's body, otherwise it would have been all up with them. But presumably he didn't, and the priests were able stealthily to transfer her huge sarcophagus to its new resting place. Imagine their panic when they discovered (they were probably working at night in case the pharaoh himself should see them) that it was too large to fit into the tomb properly, having been designed for a much larger chamber. They had to lower it on end down the long shaft, ram it into the tomb as best they could and stack in after it all the bits of furniture and belongings that remained after the robbery in the original tomb.

Then, no doubt in a fair panic, they hastily blocked the deep shaft to prevent any further enquiry. They must have spent the rest of their lives praying that Khufu would never find out, although they would have heaved sighs of relief when he built his Queens' pyramids almost on top of their dreadful secret.

Some four hundred years afterwards the Old Kingdom apparently collapsed in chaos and civil war, a condition which seems to have lasted some hundred and fifty years until strong pharaohs asserted themselves again and the Middle Kingdom got under way. Few records remain from this First Intermediate Period, since there was no central authority and hence nobody (except locally) whose job it was to keep records. But once the 11th Dynasty had begun and order was eventually restored throughout Egypt, the Egyptians began looking back to that black century and a half of collapse and saw it as dividing them from the previous golden age of the Old Kingdom when Egypt had been the most powerful nation in the Near East and everything had run smoothly under its god-like pharaohs. Above all, the Middle Kingdom Egyptians thought that all the evil deeds such as tomb-robberies had taken place only during the First Intermediate Period when law and order had ceased to exist although, as we have seen, that was quite untrue. There had always been tomb-robberies, right from the beginning of the 1st Dynasty. By the start of the Middle Kingdom such robbery must have been commonplace.

Two Middle Kingdom scribes, Ipu-wer and Neferti, described the total chaos of this previous period as if they had been eye-witnesses, although in fact they were looking back.

'The robber is now the rich man,' wrote Ipu-wer mournfully. 'Men sit in the bushes until the traveller comes in order to take away his burden and steal what he carries. He is beaten with sticks and wrongfully killed. If only men ceased to exist, that there were no conception, no birth! . . . The children of nobles are dashed against walls. Children of the neck (i.e. babes in arms) are laid out in the desert. Noble ladies suffer like maidservants and nobles are themselves in the workhouse . . .

'I show you the land all topsy-turvy,' wailed Neferti. 'Men make metal arrows and laugh with the laughter of madmen . . . I show you the son as a foe, the brother as an enemy, and a man killing his own father . . . Everything good has disappeared.'

It is true that they were describing a situation which was safely in the past, but it must have seemed that the over-turning of everything sacred had caused evils which could never be put right again. Even the pharaoh himself was no longer so mysterious and untouchable.

'Behold, something has been done which never happened before: the King has been taken away by poor men. He who was buried as a divine falcon is now laid on a simple bier. What

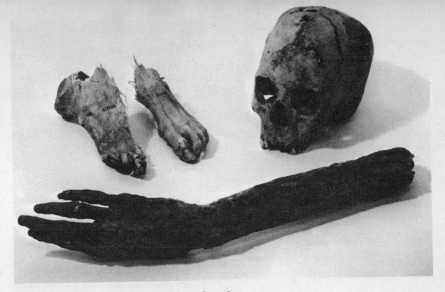

Fragments of a Middle Kingdom female mummy

the pyramid hid has become empty.'

Indeed, the old tombs had been abandoned by priests and guards. They were crumbling with age and damage caused by people demolishing them for the stone blocks with which to build their own tombs. The money left for their upkeep had finally run out. Decent burials during this First Intermediate Period must have been few and far between. Bodies were probably simply tossed into the Nile or laid out, like the 'children of the neck', in the desert just as the poor had always been.

'To whom can I speak today?' asks an anonymous writer from this period in an extraordinary lament normally called *The Man Who Was Tired of Life*. 'I am laden with wretchedness for lack of an intimate friend. To whom can I speak today? The sin which treads the earth, it has no end.'

This moment in their history must have deeply disturbed the Egyptian people since it proved that what they had thought of as a wealthy and secure state was capable of becoming poor and decadent. It badly shook their confidence in the old ways, and changed their attitude towards their pharaohs. Whereas

the Old Kingdom pharaoh had been a god on earth so dangerous to approach that all his chief ministers had to be found
from among his own family, the pharaohs of the Middle Kingdom were actually referred to as 'Good Shepherds'. They were
still the sons of the god Re, but they were somewhat friendlier
towards their people and had more contact with them.

But their belief in the afterlife had not changed; and since it
seemed that the huge pyramid and the magic power of the
god-kings had not been enough to prevent tomb-robberies, the
royal architects of the Middle Kingdom decided to alter the
design of the tombs. Whereas in the Old Kingdom any robber
knew that the entrance to a pyramid was always in its north
face, his counterpart in the Middle Kingdom could not be so
sure. The architects now often put the entrance some distance
from the pyramid itself and camouflaged it ingeniously. There
was an open attempt to try to beat the robbers simply by out-
thinking them, and the royal architects often excelled themselves in constructing ever more elaborate blind alleys and
mazes to protect the inner tomb. The Middle Kingdom
pharaohs also moved their capital city to the Faiyum region –
away from the Old Kingdom capital of Memphis, so they now
had a new – and hopefully better – royal cemetery.

The Middle Kingdom lasted some three hundred years until
there was another breakdown of government known as the
Second Intermediate Period. Presumably the robberies had
continued as before; for by the time that the 18th Dynasty
began the New Kingdom (in about 1567 B.C.), it was belatedly
decided that pyramids were not the best form of tomb since
they were so painfully obvious. Because the capital city had
moved once more and was now at Thebes in an area of country
with cliff formations on either side of the Nile, what more
natural than to choose the cliffs themselves as a giant monument?
Thus began the era of rock-cut tombs (sometimes known as
hypogea (from the Greek meaning 'underground') which were
simply hacked out of the soft limestone cliffs.

Behind one range of these cliffs which flanked the Nile at

Thebes there lay a rocky valley. Even nowadays it is hard to reach on foot, and on the face of it there is little to tempt one to desert the green banks of the river and struggle up in the blazing heat through the bare rock and loose shale. At least, so the pharaohs of the New Kingdom must have thought, for they chose this remote valley on the West Bank of the Nile as their new cemetery. From the city on the East bank the bodies were ferried across on royal barges and carried in processions led by priests up the rocky track which led to the Valley of the Kings.

The cutting of rock tombs was very carefully organized. First of all, it had to be done in the strictest secrecy so that as few people as possible knew where they were. The royal architect Ineny, who was in charge of cutting the tombs for Amenophis I and Tuthmosis I a little before 1500 B.C., wrote: 'I supervised the carving of the tomb of His Majesty in a solitary place, none seeing, none hearing.'

However, since a rock tomb might take anything up to two years to cut and needed gangs of labourers, it was impossible to keep it a complete secret. Although the workmen were carefully checked and made to live in strict isolation in a village near the site (they even had to send their laundry down to be done in Thebes), and although they often built mud-brick walls around the tomb entrance while work was in progress so that it could not be seen, more than enough people must have known the exact location to make it inevitable that the robberies would continue.

They did. True, the new rock-cut tombs worked for a while, in that thefts were less frequent. But by the end of the 20th Dynasty – about 1100 B.C. – they occurred more and more often until they became an open scandal. It was quite clear that the thieves were being helped by the very people who were supposed to be protecting the tombs: the priests and the necropolis police.

This time there was a new reason why the robbers were so desperate. By 1150 B.C. the Bronze Age in Egypt was over because iron was being mined in quantity in foreign territories.

Iron was a much more useful metal; but unfortunately Egypt had few iron ore deposits, so suddenly the country had found itself forced to import it from the Hittites, among others. This was humiliating. It also meant the partial collapse of the Egyptian economy. Everything began to cost more, and the already poor became wretched. Practically nobody had any money, so it was inevitable that people would sooner or later turn once more to the great hoards of gold and silver buried in the hills with their dead pharaohs. The curious thing is that when they did the economy began improving. The re-circulation of all that buried wealth largely eased the Egyptians' financial problem.

It is from this period that the best record of tomb-robberies dates. By a stroke of luck several papyri have survived describing the trials of thieves who were caught. What emerges from these records is a picture of widespread corruption among many people in official positions. Since the robberies continued year after year and since those responsible for preventing them remained in their jobs, there had to be people in high places taking bribes.

And so there were. One of the best papyri to come down dates from the 16th year of the reign of King Ramesses IX, some time before 1120 B.C. In July or August of that year there was an official investigation into tomb-robberies which had recently taken place in the Valley of the Kings. Among those who played leading roles in the drama that followed was the Vizier Kha-em-Wast, who was acting for the pharaoh. Under him in terms of rank came the two mayors of East and West Thebes, Paser and Paweraa, who were responsible for their respective territories on opposite banks of the Nile. Last but not least came the two accused: Pai-Kharu the coppersmith and Amen-pa-nefer the stonemason – ordinary working men who were unlucky enough to get caught up in a huge quarrel between two Government officials.

It seems that the City's Mayor, Paser, one day wrote to the Vizier saying that his colleague over the river, the Mayor of the

The Abbott tomb-robbery papyrus containing judicial proceedings against Theban tomb robbers

necropolis, was not doing his job properly. There had, said Paser, been far too much tomb-robbery going on in Paweraa's patch. His police were obviously no use or else there was something much more sinister going on.

It is impossible to say now what Paser's motives were in thus informing on his colleague. Perhaps he had a long-standing feud with Paweraa; perhaps he genuinely felt shocked at the desecration of the tombs; or perhaps he even had dark motives of his own (such as wanting Paweraa removed so he could cut himself in on the spoils).

Either way, Paweraa was forced into opening an official investigation into these allegations against himself. The Vizier drew up a commission of enquiry with Paweraa at its head, and on a blistering summer day they all trailed round the necropolis at Thebes looking for evidence that the tombs had been tampered with. Paser had alleged fourteen specific robberies in his charges against Paweraa but the perspiring officials could confirm only three: the tombs of one king and two queens.

Admittedly, they did find that 'all' the nobles' tombs had been broken into and damaged but the commission played this down in their report. Nobles didn't count the same as royalty, so Paser's allegations were found to be more or less untrue.

Nevertheless, they *had* found three robberies on his territory so to be on the safe side Paweraa decided to haul in some petty criminals and pin the charges on them. They would be useful scapegoats. So musing, he and his commission climbed into their barge and crossed the Nile back to the city where he handed the Vizier his report.

The wretched scapegoats were rounded up at once and promptly 'examined'. 'Examination' in Egyptian court accounts always means the same thing: torture. The procedure was to punctuate the cross-examination of the prisoner with beatings on the soles of the feet or brisk twistings of arms or feet, the idea being that if he were trying to hide something it would induce him to speak up and that if he were entirely innocent and knew nothing then it was best to make sure.

So Pai-Kharu the coppersmith and Amen-pa-nefer the stonemason were 'examined' rather painfully. Pai-Kharu must have decided that it would hurt less to keep talking, so he admitted that he *had* once done a job in the necropolis – only a little robbery, though, and all of two years ago. The next day the commission re-assembled and took the blindfolded Pai-Kharu back across the Nile to the scene of his 'crime'. There, he was asked to identify the tombs he had robbed. But Pai-Kharu could only point out two places: one was an unused tomb while the other was a necropolis workman's hut. It looked as though he had made up the story to avoid further beating. But to make quite certain he was 'examined with a very severe examination' on the spot, but nothing else could be learned from him. The members of the commission wandered about, peering at various tomb doors and finding that the seals were intact. So they called it a day and trooped back across the river to the capital, no doubt thinking that Paser had been making a lot of fuss about nothing.

That night Paweraa organized a huge demonstration in
Thebes in praise of himself. The cheering crowds were urged
to chant slogans such as 'Amun bless our Mayor' and, a bit
later on, 'Down with the lying scum Paser'.

The cries of the mob rose into the velvety Egyptian night.
Hearing them, Paser decided that there was only one thing to
do, so he immediately laid fresh accusations against Paweraa.
On learning this, Paweraa marched into the Vizier's office and
demanded a new commission of enquiry to clear him once and
for all. 'I report these accusations to my Lord,' he said piously,
'for it would indeed be a crime for one in my position to hear
something but to hide it.' He then added craftily that if Paser
had known about these 'robberies' all along and had been
halfway honest or responsible he would have told the Vizier
himself.

Somewhat wearily the Vizier formed a new team of enquiry,
this time heading it himself. The next day he presided over
court to hear the accusations. Paser was there to make his
charges again, but before he could do so the Vizier hopelessly
biased the proceedings against him by pointing out sarcastically
that he, the Vizier, had been present when they had all
inspected the necropolis on the previous day, and they had
found nothing wrong. Was Paser perhaps hinting that they were
all blind? Then the Vizier waved a hand at the prisoners, who
had no doubt been bastinadoed on the soles of their feet overnight whenever their warders grew bored. 'Let's hear what the
coppersmith has to say again.'

At last, Pai-Kharu got painfully to his feet and stuck to his
story. Case dismissed. Mayor Paser had lost practically before
he had begun. The prisoners hobbled away free men, and
Paser was officially reprimanded.

From this moment the wretched Mayor of Thebes disappears
from history. No more references to him have ever been found.
He may have been sacked from the job, he may have committed
suicide out of a sense of sheer injustice, or he may simply have
moved from Thebes and gone to earth somewhere a long way

away where the people had never heard of ex-Mayor Paser.

The crafty Paweraa, however, was still Mayor and Chief of the necropolis police in Western Thebes seventeen years later and, as J. A. Wilson notes in *The Culture of Ancient Egypt*, they were seventeen years in which the tomb robberies in his district continued to increase. Fifteen months after this trial, one of the tombs in the Queens' Valley [near the Valley of the Kings] was found smashed to bits by robbers. In all the documents of the investigation there was not a single defendant of high position. Only the little men, the stonemasons and coppersmiths and farmers, were caught. Why?

The answer was simple. One of those who made the later raid in the Queen's Valley turned out to be none other than the stonemason Amen-pa-nefer who had been arrested and tried with Pai-Kharu. He had led his gang of seven to loot the tomb of Sobkemsaf one night and they had come away with forty pounds of gold, an immense sum. This they divided into eight shares before crossing the Nile back to the capital under cover of darkness. However, somebody must have talked. Amen-pa-nefer was caught and imprisoned. No doubt he was about to be 'severely examined' when he had the bright idea of using his five-pound share of the gold to buy his way out of prison. Once released, he tracked down his gang who, being gentlemen, pooled some of their gold to make up what their leader had lost. Then they all went back to a life of crime, safe in the knowledge that every official had his price. It was during that raid on Sobkemsaf's tomb that Amen-pa-nefer stole the magnificent heart scarab now in the British Museum (see Chapter 3 and the illustration on p. 136).

About a century later the authorities finally took action. Most of the surviving royal mummies of the 18th to the 20th Dynasties were moved from their tombs for a secret re-burial in the tomb of Queen Inhapy behind the Deir el Bahri Temple on the West Bank at Thebes. There they were unceremoniously stacked up like so many logs. Since the bodies had long ago been plundered they had no more valuables on them and so lay forgotten for over three thousand years.

Strangely enough – since it was robbers who had made it necessary to hide all those dead kings in a secret pit – it was robbers who eventually discovered them again. The story now shifts to late last century, a leap of three millennia, and takes place in the comparatively modern world. Yet it is the same old story of tomb-robbery which has much in common with the case of Paser and Paweraa back in the 20th Dynasty.

Towards the end of the last century a small but regular trickle of papyri, Canopic jars, *shabtis* and similar things began turning up for sale in Egypt. This was the great age of Egyptology, and its pioneers were extremely anxious that as little historical evidence as possible should vanish into the hands of private citizens. It was vital to preserve everything that was unearthed so that scholars could see the objects first before turning them over to museums. The great French Egyptologist, Gaston Maspero, came across some of these hitherto unknown relics up for private sale and, worried, immediately launched into an impressive piece of detective work to find out where they had come from.

> From 1878 I was able to confirm that the Arabs had discovered one or several of the still unknown Royal Tombs of the 21st Dynasty. In March and April 1881 I tried to trace them. It wasn't a question of discreet personal enquiry – more of winkling out the *fellahin*'s secret by force or by trickery . . .

Maspero finally discovered that the principal sellers of these objects were two brothers living in the village of Qurneh, near the site of the Valley of the Kings. They were Ahmed and Mohammed Abd er-Rassul. There was a third man involved, Mustafa Ayat; but since he turned out to be the acting British, Belgian and Russian Consul in Luxor he had diplomatic immunity and hence could not be touched. Maspero decided to concentrate his attack on the Abd er-Rassul brothers.

He had Ahmed hauled in by the police and interrogated –

evidently by methods not much different from those their ancestors had used during their 'severe examinations'. The case was heard before Daud Pasha, the provincial Governor. It was a bizarre scene. According to some sources the Governor was suffering agonies from a skin complaint and presided over the court while immersed up to his neck in a huge jar of water. Nevertheless, Daud Pasha's sufferings were nothing compared with those of Ahmed er-Rassul who, it is claimed, years later still bore the scars of 'beatings, ropes and heated iron pots over the head'.

But Ahmed stuck it out and said nothing, and finally they were obliged to free him. It seems that he staggered home, much bruised and scorched, and had a considerable argument with his brother Mohammed and the rest of his family. Ahmed claimed that since he'd undergone all that torture but had kept their secret, he ought to get a guaranteed half share of all future booty instead of his usual fifth. Otherwise, he said, he would go to Daud Pasha and tell him where they were looting. The family objected violently to this attempt at blackmail which – had they called his bluff – would have led to the end of their income and lengthy prison sentences. For a month or so the brothers were locked in a family feud which became common knowledge throughout the area. It was a classic case of thieves falling out.

Realizing that sooner or later the authorities were bound to hear about it Mohammed himself went in secret to Daud Pasha on 25 June 1881 and said that he would tell all as long as he was guaranteed immunity. He was, and he did. On 6 July he personally led a collection of Egyptologists and officials to the entrance of the unknown tomb he and his brother had discovered. What they found became known as the 'Deir el Bahri cache' and the news of it went round the world.

It was one of the most important archaeological discoveries of all time. Somehow, while grubbing near the Valley of the Kings, the Abd er-Rassul brothers had blundered on that long-forgotten tomb of Queen Inhapy. It must have been a strange moment when the Egyptologists' lanterns shone on the stacks of mummies. Émile Brugsch, one of the Egyptologists, said later that 'it all seemed like a dream, something impossible to believe'. Maspero agreed. 'Like him, I ask myself if I am not dreaming when I see and touch the bodies of so many rulers of whom we thought we would only ever know the name.'

For there before their eyes were the actual bodies of many of the most legendary pharaohs: Seqenenre II, Ahmose, Tuthmosis III, Seti I, Ramesses II . . . It turned out that the Abd er-Rassul brothers had kept their secret so well that the inhabitants of nearby Luxor and Qurneh were as amazed as the Europeans. As the news spread, so did wild rumours of caskets stuffed with gold; and in case looters were attracted to the scene it was decided to move the whole mass burial to the safety of Cairo. Two hundred Arabs were recruited and put to work.

On 11 July everything was moved to Luxor on the Nile for embarkation. Mummies, coffins and furniture were all wrapped in sheets, once more warmed by the sun after more than three thousand years of cool darkness. Three days later the steamer *Menshiya* arrived, loaded up and left at full speed for Cairo with its cargo of pharaohs. As it chugged away peasants came running out of their villages and lined the river bank to pay tribute to their former kings. 'Women wailed and tore their hair; men solemnly fired their shotguns into the air. It was a traditional funeral. The kings who had lain at Thebes for three thousand years were now leaving for ever.'

Yet even this stately pageant had its last note of farce. When the royal mummies arrived in Cairo they had to be assessed for taxation, as the law required for all goods brought into the city. The problem was, how did one classify a mummy? It wasn't meat, and it wasn't cloth, and it wasn't an antique object made of wood or stone. Finally someone hit on an answer, and the greatest rulers of the ancient world at last entered the Egyptian capital classified as dried fish. It only added to the irony that this classification unwittingly gave a more accurate account of their embalming than if they had been called 'mummies'.

Back at Qurneh the informant, Mohammed Abd er-Rassul, was rewarded with £500 sterling – an immense sum – and appointed Chief of the Antiquities Service guards in the necropolis. But he soon paid back his new masters. In 1891 he revealed to Maspero's successor the burial place of the Priests of Amun, another mass burial on which he and his brothers had stumbled earlier. In 1898 V. Loret, an Egyptologist, made his own unaided discovery of another royal cache in the tomb of Amenophis II in the Valley of the Kings. Here were all the missing pharaohs: Merenptah, Tuthmosis IV and Amenophis III. Amenophis II's mummy was left in the tomb; the others were removed to Cairo. Two years later the tomb guards were overpowered, the tomb was entered and Amenophis II's mummy was stripped. It was widely believed that the Abd er-Rassuls were deeply involved in this affair.

As for Mohammed's brother Ahmed, it seems that, like Amen-pa-nefer, he went back to tomb robbery once the dust of the original trial had settled. To this day, a century later, Abd er-Rassuls still live in the village of Qurneh and still hold considerable influence in the archaeology of the Valley of the Kings. A few years ago one was granted permission to excavate in the tomb of Seti I. And although this remote village has no visible means of support, it appears to be not badly off. Many an innocent tourist must have wondered how the villagers manage to earn a living nowadays. If they knew anything about the tomb robbers of the past they would realize that ancient traditions die very hard. . . .

Thus it is that robbery has played such an important role in Egyptology. It was simple robbery which partly dictated the history of tomb design in ancient Egypt, from gigantic pyramids to anonymous holes in the rock. And although vast quantities of priceless relics must have been lost for ever through the thieves' activities, we do owe the robbers several back-handed debts of gratitude. But for them we would certainly not have so many royal mummies.

6

AMARNA, TUTANKHAMUN AND TANIS

It is ironic that the Egyptian pharaoh whose name is most familiar to the general public today and who is most associated with the discovery of fabulous treasure should in fact have been a minor king of little real importance. It is not even certain that Tutankhamun's fabulous treasure was at all fabulous by Egyptian standards; indeed, there is enough evidence for some Egyptologists to have suggested that the priests who buried him deliberately insulted him by putting so few valuables in his tomb.

Tutankhamun cannot be left out of any account of mummies, since his is the only nearly-intact royal burial from the first twenty dynasties that has ever been found, and even it was twice broken into by tomb-robbers. Plenty of royal mummies have survived in, for example, the Deir el Bahri cache. But they were re-burials: the plundered bodies were re-wrapped but were not replaced in their own coffins, let alone with all their possessions. Instead, they were stacked up in anonymous heaps as if they had been mummified cats or birds in an animal cemetery. There were a few original grave-goods in the cache: some *shabtis* and the odd Canopic jar; but the whole re-burial was a hurried expedient by priests who probably feared divine retribution for the robbers' impiety.

The nearest thing to an intact royal burial from the start of Egyptian history until Tutankhamun himself was that of Queen Tiye's parents, Yuya and Thuya. But neither Yuya nor Thuya was royal by birth. Yuya was 'a prophet of Min' and 'an over-seer of horses' while Thuya was 'chief lady of Amun's harem', as an inscription in their tomb at Thebes describes them. Their daughter Tiye married the pharaoh, Amenophis III, which made them close enough to the royal family to be accorded a marvellous funeral. Nevertheless, theirs was not a royal burial.

After Tutankhamun we have a handful of intact royal burials: those of the 21st and 22nd Dynasties at Tanis. But they were far more modest affairs, and Tutankhamun remains the only example ever discovered of an almost complete royal burial in the traditional grand manner of ancient Egypt, although as we shall see it is possible that even this was a pale imitation of the splendours of previous dynasties.

There is another reason why Tutankhamun should be included in a book which is primarily about mummies. The exact genealogy of his family is far from clear, because for political and other reasons the royal family was forced into a confusing round of intermarriage and incest. This makes it very difficult to determine who was related to whom and in what way; but recently tests on Tutankhamun's mummy have gone some way towards making things a bit clearer. To understand Tutankhamun's style of burial, his complex blood-relationships and his place in Egyptian (if not Egyptological) history, it is necessary to go back a generation to his predecessor Akhenaten, arguably the most mysterious pharaoh of ancient Egypt.

The dynasty of Tutankhamun and Akhenaten was the 18th – the first in the so-called 'New Kingdom' which followed the expulsion of the Hyksos at the end of the Second Intermediate Period. The early kings of this dynasty secured the achievements of the Theban princes who had overthrown their foreign dominators by chasing the Hyksos into Palestine. They re-united Egypt and firmly re-established her frontiers. In doing so these pharaohs discovered that it was not very difficult to go on and conquer the small city-states in the Middle East and generally expand their sphere of influence abroad. Egypt thus changed from a state into an empire, setting up all sorts of new trading links and diplomatic relations with foreign rulers. Indeed, Akhenaten's grandfather Tuthmosis IV had taken a Mitannian princess into his harem for diplomatic reasons. Mitanni was an Indo-European empire on the headwaters of the Euphrates which had for a long time been vying with Egypt for control over Syria. The Mitannians were great horsemen and used chariots in battle – a way of fighting which was then unfamiliar to the Egyptians and which made the Mitannians a considerable threat to Egypt's military power. Finally, both parties must have decided that coming to an agreement was preferable to a long drawn-out series of wars, so they made a pact which entailed the pharaoh taking a member of the Mitannian royal family back to Egypt for a diplomatic marriage.

In order to administer their empire and to cope with the new prosperity which the trading brought them, the Egyptians had to improve their bureaucratic and governmental system. The country began to show at home all those signs of increased power which have since become familiar elsewhere: a large civil service, endless paper-work, files and records; much legislation and red tape. As the civil government became centralized there also appears to have been an attempt to 'rationalize' the state religions. This may not have been a conscious decision on anybody's part so much as a popular response among the administrative classes to the new re-ordering of Egypt which needed to make overall sense of its numerous and conflicting cults.

Whatever the reason, it seems that the cult of the sun – which ever since the Old Kingdom had been extremely important in Egypt – began to dominate all the others. Ever since the 4th Dynasty the pharaohs had referred to themselves as 'Sons of Re'; perhaps now their new empire and magnificence seemed to support the idea of *le roi soleil* ('Sun-King') even more strongly as the pharaoh beamed his influence down upon his

159

foreign territories.

By the time of Amenophis III, in the middle of the 18th Dynasty, Egypt was prosperous and stable enough for the pharaoh to be able to devote time and money almost exclusively to large-scale architectural projects and patronage of the arts. He built great temples such as that at Luxor which was dedicated to the supreme god of the Egyptian empire, Amen-Re. Amen-Re was the nearest the Egyptians came to having a single god who could unify their different beliefs. Thebes, the empire's capital, had since the Middle Kingdom been the seat of the Amun cult, which held that Amun was the 'Hidden One' manifest in the wind and in breath as the mysterious source of life in men and animals. Yet Thebes, like the rest of Egypt, also believed in the power of Re, the sun-god who so obviously ruled the seasons, which in turn regulated their lives. Gradually, therefore, the two gods had merged into a duality, the double god Amen-Re, who was neither one nor the other but both at once. (Conceptually, there is something of a parallel in this with the Christian notion of the Trinity.) It was no coincidence that the Mitannians also worshipped a sun-god, and no doubt a relationship between the two nations which involved royal intermarriage might also involve the strengthening of a common religious belief.

This new dual god had come into conceptual being at the expense of Amun, who had once stood as one of the most significant of the Egyptians' gods. Sometime during the 18th Dynasty the balance of belief began – in certain quarters at any rate – to shift in favour of the sun-god. More specifically, a cult grew up for worshipping the Aten, which was the solar disc itself. Under Tuthmosis IV this cult began to gain importance; it gained more under Amenophis III but only became official when his son by Queen Tiye came to the throne.

How son succeeded father is still not precisely known. It seems that Amenophis III took the young prince to be his co-regent until his death. That is, for some years they shared the throne while the older man presumably instructed his son in the elements of governing the empire. Yet it was probably clear from quite early on that the younger man was something of a rebel, especially in his religious beliefs. He evidently made strenuous efforts to raise the worship of the Aten to the status of supreme state religion, and this must inevitably have led to considerable problems and embarrassment for the royal family. They were, after all, ruling from the royal palace at Thebes, which was also the traditional seat of the cult of Amun. Any effort to raise the Aten at the expense of Amun would have met with instant resistance from the powerful priests who, up until then, had been the unchallenged administrators of the state religion.

We can only guess what actually happened. One theory is that the young prince – who as co-regent had taken on the title of Amenophis IV – made himself so unpopular in Thebes that his father had virtually to tell him to pack his bags, and go and play sun-gods in the desert as far away as possible. Amenophis III was a sick man and he would hardly have wanted the peace of his declining years upset by a religious fanatic in the family, establishing a rival cult and creating hostility and resistance wherever he went.

So the young Amenophis IV left Thebes and tried to find a suitable place for the centre of the Aten cult with which he was so obsessed. He later claimed to have been divinely guided when he hit on a site halfway between Thebes and Memphis, and there, as soon as his father died, he established his new capital which he named Akhetaten, or 'the horizon of the Aten'. (The modern name for the site of his capital is Tell el Amarna, and so his reign is known as the 'Amarna Period'.) Sometime during the first few years of his reign he broke still further with tradition by changing his name from Amenophis – with its association with Amun – to Akhenaten, which can be translated either as 'useful to the Aten' or 'effective spirit of the Aten'.

Akhenaten has been described as the world's first monotheist – that is, somebody who believes in only one god. This is not correct, however; strictly speaking he was a henotheist, believ-

ing in a chief god but also in other more minor deities. He dis-
approved of Amun because Amun threatened the Aten's
supremacy. So long as the other gods were inferior to the Aten
he had no objection to them. In order to establish the Aten as
unquestionably the chief of Egypt's gods, Akhenaten embarked
on a single-minded campaign which involved no less than the
setting up of a new religion and an entire new culture. This
would have been a remarkable enough ambition on the part of
any ruler at any time in history; but for a pharaoh of Egypt, a
nation that could not bear change and almost lacked the very
concept, it was the wildest form of revolution.

But this was not the only way in which Akhenaten was extraordinary, and part of the mystery which surrounds him is that
concerning his peculiar physical appearance. We do not have
a mummy we can identify as Akhenaten's, but we do have the
art of the Amarna Period, which – like everything else about
the reign of this pharaoh – broke entirely new ground. Egyptian
painting and sculpture, which had traditionally been highly
formal and conservative in its obedience to long-established
convention, suddenly became freer, expressive and often un-
ashamedly emotional.

It is true that, like any new artistic style or social movement,
it did not suddenly spring into being from nothing. We must
reject all notions of history which consider a single individual
responsible for successfully launching an entirely self-generated
revolution, whether political or artistic. The right conditions
must exist first; and in fact the features which so strongly
characterize the art of Amarna had mostly been present during
the reign of Amenophis III and may clearly be seen in much of
the work of his period. Thus the social conditions had already
been fulfilled which made both the art and the heresy of
Amarna possible. It merely needed someone with enough power
to espouse and cultivate it. As pharaoh, Akhenaten had the
power; but what is so remarkable is that he should have used
this power to break with tradition. A pharaoh breaking a
tradition was a contradiction in terms: a pharaoh *was* tradition,

he embodied changelessness.

And yet as king he altered the very image of royalty. Instead of the rigid figures of pharaohs whom sculptors always portrayed as slim young men, regardless of their bulk and decrepitude, there were pictures and carvings of Akhenaten slumped on his throne with a grotesquely long face and chin, pronounced breasts, a pear-shaped belly, fat hips and thighs and thin stick-like arms and legs. Egyptologists believe that these features, although perhaps exaggerated for effect, did represent a likeness of the king and that it must have been entirely Akhenaten's idea to adopt such brutal realism at his own expense. Perhaps it was in line with Akhenaten's governing principle of *maat*, which we can tentatively translate here as Truth.

It is part of Akhenaten's achievement that he so quickly inspired enough artists, sculptors and masons to establish this new art and, indeed, provide all the designs, decorations and stonework for his brand-new capital city. It was a new aesthetic movement, and a heady sense of liberation must have swept through the artisans of Akhetaten. The paintings in tombs and elsewhere took on a new life. Instead of the static friezes of people in flat outline there was movement and a naturalistic effect. Girls stooped, heads turned, hands waved, stags leaped in thickets, people kissed. The bold – and until then unthinkable – way of painting the pharaoh as a man, rather than as the idealized symbol of a god, caught on. Other people in Amarna art, and not just members of the royal family, began to be depicted realistically and even to resemble the pharaoh's strange physique.

So odd does Akhenaten look in some of his representations that it has been suggested he was suffering from some kind of disease. When he is pictured with his queen, the famously beautiful Nefertiti, it is sometimes impossible to tell which is which. The king has the same feminine physique, and some of the huge statues of Akhenaten which survive show him without any genitals at all. Diagnoses range from the possibility that he might have been a woman to the rather more likely surmise

Nefertiti, wife of Akhenaten

that he suffered from Fröhlich's syndrome, a condition resulting from the malfunction of the pituitary gland which controls growth. Typically, Fröhlich's syndrome is characterized by fatness, physical sluggishness, and retarded sexual development.

The problem about this diagnosis is that a sufferer is almost certain to be impotent, and Akhenaten is unique among the pharaohs in the manner in which he portrayed himself as a family man. He had six daughters by Nefertiti and frequently appears in pictures with them. If they were not his own children then it is barely possible that his father Amenophis III might have sired one or more of them, since he was alive two years after the youngest was born. Perhaps also the mother was not

Nefertiti in all six cases. But the hieroglyphs insist that they were Akhenaten's own children, and it seems reasonable to suppose that if he had needed to conceal his impotence he would have found a male infant to pass off as his, because with six daughters and no son the throne was left without a male heir.

This was not Akhenaten's only problem, though, since he was meanwhile facing severe political opposition outside Amarna. Setting up the machinery of a new state religion was an enormous and vastly expensive project, and to pay for it Akhenaten virtually had to declare war on Amunism and its priests at Thebes in order to dispossess them. Only by doing this could he take over for the Aten the fleets of ships, the thousands of acres of prime farmland, the huge army of priests, the bureaucracy and administration owned and run by the erstwhile state religion. As can be imagined, this was not

Two of the daughters of Nefertiti and Akhenaten. This wall painting demonstrates the new artistic freedom of the Amarna period.

popular with the priests of Amun or the nobles and ruling classes of Thebes and elsewhere in Egypt.

It would have been particularly unpopular with the priests whose living depended on the cult of Amun and who decided to remain loyal to it. At the very least they would have been much inconvenienced by the sudden withdrawal of their 'perks', for it must be remembered that all the offerings left on the offering-tables were retrieved by the priests after a decent interval and kept by them. The offering ceremonies were frequent enough for the bread not to go stale nor the beer flat, and the huge quantities of both contractually required by the better class of dead person must have made any priest and his family decidedly fat. Theology allowed that the 'spirit' of the food could pass into the 'spirit' of the divine Osiris 'x' or God 'y'; practicality provided that the food, once it had been offered, was removed and distributed among the priests according to a set system. Thus the god was fed, and also those responsible for feeding him. However, it was quite clear that not every priest bothered to offer the food he knew he was anyway going to eat. Thus a text in the Temple of Edfu reminds the priesthood that 'one lives on the food of the gods; but this is always food which leaves the altar *after the god is satisfied*'.

Akhenaten, whose new cult seemed likely to damage irreparably a very comfortable living for a great many people, was no doubt looked upon as a wild and dangerous lunatic in his strange new city miles from anywhere, even if he *was* the pharaoh. This was the heart of the problem. Pharaohs were supposed to rule, and Akhenaten was an absentee pharaoh living in a kind of metropolitan folly that was a world of his own, utterly remote from the affairs of state which became more and more pressing the more they were ignored. Probably only the common people were left unmoved by this, since Atenism and their pharaoh's obsession with it would have remained as incomprehensible and inaccessible as any other theological argument. For them it was something for priests and pharaohs to bother with, and several archaeological finds even in the city of the Aten itself show that they went on with their own curious array of gods and beliefs pretty much as they always had done.

In the twelfth year of Akhenaten's reign Nefertiti seems to vanish, which is to say there is no further mention of her in the records, and it is most likely that she simply died. Yet the name which is now linked with Akhenaten's on monuments, in place of his wife's, is that of a certain Smenkhkare. Smenkhkare was either Akhenaten's half- or his full brother, it is not certain which. They were both definitely the sons of Amenophis III (who in any case married his own daughter), but nobody can be sure if they shared the same mother. Akhenaten's mother was Queen Tiye; but who else's mother was she? In Tutankhamun's tomb there was a locket containing a snippet of hair clearly labelled as belonging to Queen Tiye, so it seems quite likely that she was indeed his mother as well, and that he, Smenkhkare and Akhenaten were all full brothers.

When Akhenaten was about thirty he took the young Smenkhkare as his co-regent. It is obvious that their relationship was extremely close: indeed, certain hints and pieces of art-work, such as the statuette of the 'kissing kings' in the Louvre, have led people to suggest that they were lovers. However that may be, the order of events following Smenkhkare's accession to the shared throne is unclear. Smenkhkare died either just before or very shortly after Akhenaten and is believed to have been buried in what is today known as Tomb 55 at Biban el Moluk near Thebes, a few yards from where Tutankhamun was to be buried some nine years later. This tomb has caused endless confusion, since most of the cartouches identifying the body were defaced or erased at some unspecified date. Guesses as to the identity of the occupant have ranged from Queen Tiye to Smenkhkare and Akhenaten himself. However, the bones of the mummy (the body and wrappings having been badly rotted by damp) have recently been subjected to very close examination by pathologists, and opinion now seems to favour Smenkhkare. The scientists did establish that not only did the skull bear a close resemblance to Tutankhamun's, which in turn has some of the distinctive shape familiar from Amarna art, but that the two had shared the same blood-groups.

The death of Akhenaten took place in his 17th regnal year, but little more is known either about what happened to his body or about the political upheavals caused by his death. The throne passed to the only remaining male of the dynasty, the nine-year-old, whose name at that stage was Tutankhaten. Some people assume that at this point the Theban hierarchy decided that the time was ripe to bring the so-called Amarna heresy to an end now that its founder was safely dead; to bury the Aten, bring what remained of the royal family back to Thebes, restore Amun to his rightful place as supreme god of Egypt and try to rescue the State from the edge of political disaster. According to this theory the boy pharaoh and his advisers returned to Thebes and were given a guarded welcome back into the fold. Tutankhaten changed his name to Tutankhamun, and the ill-starred city of Akhetaten was abandoned. Its valuables were removed, its wooden gates and door-posts were stripped out and taken to Thebes (large trees were rare in Egypt so most wood for building was imported and consequently of high value), its inhabitants moved out and it was left to the wind and the jackals and the encroaching desert.

Tutankhamun reigned nine years, during which time the remaining priests of Amun no doubt did their utmost to repair the damage which had been done to their religion. Much of the powerful administrative machinery had been press-ganged by Akhenaten into the service of the Aten, and it would have been the work of years to reverse all the changes. Of the priests, some had readily transferred their allegiance to Akhenaten's new religion, whereas the rest had gone into hiding and kept their heads down. Yet although the Aten had for a while been the state deity the cult itself had been sited almost exclusively in a remote part of Egypt and had been largely irrelevant to the common people. When Akhenaten died so did Atenism, since it had been practically exclusive to the royal family and court. The priests of Amun and the Theban hierarchy must have wondered how much could be expected of Tutankhamun. Not only was he a mere boy, but he was a blood-relative – if not full brother – to Akhenaten himself, and probably still retained happy memories of a hermetically close family life at Amarna.

However, to prove himself loyal to Amun and as if to renounce his family allegiances, Tutankhamun added to the Amun temple at Luxor which Amenophis III had built, as well as to Karnak. When he died he was only eighteen and the religion of Amun was still not back to its former glory. It is fairly certain that his sudden death was quite unexpected (is that hole in the side of his skull the result of a blow before or after death?) just as that of his probable brother Smenkhkare had been. And just as Smenkhkare (if it is really him in Tomb 55) had been given a woman's coffin hurriedly adapted, so Tutankhamun took over the Canopic jars that had originally been made for Smenkhkare.

What remains unfathomable is whether Tutankhamun's funeral and burial were typical or not. It all hinges on how far he had been forgiven his connections with Amarna. If the priests of Amun thought he had made suitable amends, then the treasures they sent with Tutankhamun to the other world were probably representative of the style in which any pharaoh could expect to be buried. If, on the other hand, they had never properly forgiven him his and his family's heresy, the contents of his tomb, splendid though we may think them, may have been paltry enough to be a well-calculated insult on the part of the priests.

The contents of Tutankhamun's burial have been much described and exhibited. While many Egyptologists familiar with the whole range of Egyptian art feel that his treasures represent that art past its zenith and find many of the designs rather vulgar and gaudy, it still remains the only intact burial of its kind. It is its uniqueness which partly makes it easy to overlook any aesthetic shortcomings; and the more we know about the depredations of time and tomb-robbers and the mere thirty centimetres of rock which lay between Tutankhamun's burial and the workmen constructing the tomb of Ramesses VI, the more remarkable it seems. Its greatness seems in proportion to the slenderness of the chance by which it survived, and it is easy to understand the awe of Howard Carter, its discoverer, when on the afternoon of 16 November 1922 he broke into the ante-chamber. Later, he wrote of this experience:

> With trembling hands, I made a tiny breach in the upper left-hand corner. Darkness and blank space, as far as an iron testing-rod could reach . . . Candle tests were applied as a precaution against possible foul gases, and then, widening the hole a little, I inserted the candle and peered in . . . At first I could see nothing, the hot air escaping from the chamber causing the candle to flicker. But presently, as my eyes grew accustomed to the light, details of the room emerged slowly from the mist, strange animals, statues, and gold – everywhere the glint of gold. For a moment – for an eternity it must have seemed to the others standing by, I was struck dumb; then Lord Carnarvon inquired anxiously – "Can you see anything?"
> "Yes," I replied, . . . "wonderful things. . . ."

It was one of the great moments of archaeology. The news, even more than that of the discovery of the Deir el Bahri cache near the Valley of the Kings in 1881, at once reached all parts of the world. Carter's amazement was all the greater since he had initially been prepared for disappointment. When he had cleared the rubble from the flight of sixteen stone steps and reached the tomb doorway, he could see that it had been opened and re-sealed twice, so he assumed that the tomb had been plundered like so many before. The rubble filling the corridor inside contained a tunnel large enough for a man to squeeze through, and this had been repaired with stones of a different colour.

At the end of the corridor was an ante-chamber from which

Howard Carter (left) and Lord Carnarvon who together discovered and excavated the tomb of Tutankhamun

The discovery of the stone sarcophagus of Tutankhamun. Opening the fourth shrine. Howard Carter is the kneeling figure.

led two sealed-off rooms: the annexe and the burial chamber itself and an unsealed room, the Treasury. In the walled-up doorway leading to the annexe there was an unrepaired hole, again big enough for a man but not enough to allow large objects to be brought through. In the annexe there was a considerable mess. Objects had been stacked haphazardly and overturned. There was a handful of heavy gold rings tied up in a cloth on the floor of the ante-chamber. There was a footprint (a robber's?) on one of Tutankhamun's bow-cases, and greasy fingerprints on empty vessels which had contained precious oils. All the evidence pointed to the thieves having been caught in the act. They had no time to take large objects away and the tomb was anyway too crammed for them to be able to reach the best things quickly. Instead, they had concentrated on small objects with immediate high re-sale value, such as gold rings and expensive oils; but such was their hurry to get out that they even dropped the rings. Perhaps the necropolis guards had not been well enough bribed that night and decided that they could get more by turning the thieves in. The priests made some attempt to repair the damage, re-sealed some of the holes and the burial remained forgotten for the next three thousand years.

It is obvious that the tomb is really far too small for all the objects that were crammed into it. Again, it has been suggested that it had not originally been designed for Tutankhamun at all, and not even for a pharaoh. Perhaps this was all part of the Amun priests' calculated insult, if that was what it was. The tomb might have belonged to Ay, who, as brother to Queen Tiye, had been one of Akhenaten's political advisers and who, on Tutankhamun's death, had married the late king's widow.

At any rate the burial survived what seems to have been an orgy of destruction which was launched some years afterwards during the Ramesside period and which was aimed at blotting out once and for all every trace of Akhenaten and Amarna. Wherever Akhenaten's name appeared it was chiselled out or erased. His statues were defaced, his carvings were smashed and the remains of his city further dismantled for building

The gold mask of Tutankhamun

blocks. What may have been Smenkhkare's mummy in Tomb 55 was rendered anonymous. Akhenaten's own mummy has completely disappeared and it may have suffered the worst fate possible for an Egyptian by having been burnt.

With Tutankhamun's death the 18th Dynasty virtually came to an end. It dragged on for another thirty-two years but

Tutankhamun's gilded second coffin within his stone sarcophagus in the Valley of the Kings at Thebes

the royal line was finished, and first Ay and then a general named Horemheb (who was probably married to Nefertiti's sister) became pharaoh before the first Ramesses founded a new dynasty. The extraordinary 'Amarna Period' is left as an enigma, full of unanswered and unanswerable questions. By the flimsiest chance much has survived the passage of time and deliberate destruction: a nearly-intact royal burial, the relics of a vivid artistic and religious movement, and something of the distinctive personality of the strange man who gave the movement its impetus. Nothing like Amarna had ever happened before in Egypt, and it never happened again. But tokens remain to this day which make this brief moment of Egyptian history seem more accessible to us than many far later events. The lock of his mother's hair with which Tutankhamun was buried and the portraits of affectionate family scenes at Amarna come to mind. In his book *The Egyptians* Cyril Aldred gives a further poignant instance: 'So much has the past survived at Amarna that the track, for instance, that Penhasi, the Chief Servitor of the Aten, made by his daily walk between his house and the temple may still be seen on the desert surface in the evening light.'

Likewise, Leonard Cottrell in *The Secrets of Tutankhamun* quotes Sir Alan Gardiner describing being present with Howard Carter when Carter was examining some of Tutankhamun's boxes for the first time:

"Carter opened one of these and on the top lay a beautiful ostrich-feather fan. The feathers were perfect, fluffing out just as if they had been recently plucked, and waving gently in the slight draught which came through the now-opened doorway of the sepulchre. Those feathers completely annihilated the centuries for me. It was just as if the king had been buried only a few days before. Of course in a few days they

Ostrich-feather fan

began to decay and had to be preserved in paraffin wax, but when I first saw them they were perfect; and they made on me an impression such as I had never experienced before, and never shall again."

The Ramesside period followed the reigns of Ay and Horemheb, and at the end of it most of the great tomb-robberies occurred. During the next dynasty (the 21st) the plundered mummies were re-bound and reburied in the mass grave at Deir el Bahri. Many details of the 21st Dynasty are unclear. For various reasons the power and stability which Egypt had enjoyed at the beginning of the 18th Dynasty had collapsed; the great empire dwindled, and Egypt itself became administratively split into two halves, again almost as it had been in pre-dynastic times. Upper Egypt was ruled from Thebes in the south, while Lower Egypt was ruled from a place in the Delta called Tanis. The circumstances of this split were quite different from those before the 1st Dynasty, however. There was no state of civil war. What had happened was that the Amun priesthood had regained all the power it had lost during the Amarna period and had considerably added to it. It was the priests who now virtually ruled the Theban area of Egypt with full royal consent from the pharaoh in Tanis.

It is at Tanis that the only other intact royal burials have been found, and once again the design of the tombs was dictated by the nature of the local geography. Because the Delta is so low and flat the water-table is very high. It is not possible to dig down very far without finding water, so underground tombs were out of the question. Instead, the kings of the 21st and 22nd Dynasties built their tombs above ground in simple stone structures, some of them actually incorporated into the south-west corner of the mud-brick wall surrounding the great temple of Anat which in places was as much as eighteen metres thick.

There, in 1940, the French Egyptologist Pierre Montet discovered several of these tombs intact. They were of kings such

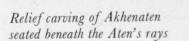

Relief carving of Akhenaten
seated beneath the Aten's rays

24431

as Psusennes, Amenemope, one of the Sheshonqs, the general
Wendjebawendjed and Prince Harnakht, a son of Sheshonq I.
The first tomb to be found was that of Osorkon II. It was a
stone-lined chamber containing four granite sarcophagi. Two
of the coffins were empty, since the tomb had been robbed;
Harnakht had been almost completely robbed but his mummy
was still there; while Psusennes' sarcophagus was quite intact.

The other five tombs were variously robbed and intact. What was striking was the difference between the burial of these pharaohs and that of their predecessors. Gone was the huge collection of grave-goods. Instead, the small tombs were comparatively stark, and it is impossible to imagine an early king of Egypt even contemplating being buried so ascetically in a mud-brick wall.

Nevertheless, considerable wealth was represented in these lesser-known Tanis burials. The coffins were of solid silver, some falcon-headed and some human-headed. They were fairly crude and massive; and although by this time silver was commoner than it had been it was still rarer than gold and therefore more valuable. There were fine gold and silver vessels, solid' gold masks and collars and a marvellous collection of jewellery: amulets, bracelets, rings, ear-rings, girdles and pectorals.

These comparatively few treasures, then, are all that is left of over three thousand years of royal burials in Egypt. Half a dozen pharaohs remain more or less as they were buried, with much pomp, 'for eternity'. The rest have vanished or have been ravaged by time and robbers. Their great wealth was looted and presumably found its way back into the economy which had supplied it in the first place. Their bodies rotted or were burnt by politicians or plunderers; they have been torn apart by impatient thieves or ground up into a powder eaten by Europeans centuries later for its supposed magical properties. When the passage of so much time is considered, though, perhaps it is surprising that anything has survived. It is certainly ironic that hardly a pharaoh with all his wealth has lasted as well as 'Ginger' with his little collection of earthenware pots and flints.

7

THE MUMMIES AND EUROPE

From the days of the early Greek historians ancient Egyptian civilization has exercised an extraordinary fascination over other cultures. Because it was such a comparatively stable and long-lived civilization, and one which had demonstrably reached a degree of great sophistication in its art and science as well as in its pre-industrial technology, even its eventual foreign rulers stood in awe of the remnants of Egypt. The early Christians of the first two centuries A.D. deeply felt the weight of what they saw as three thousand years' heathen and idolatrous culture, and aimed much of their reforming zeal at the great animal necropolises such as Saqqara. The animal deities were their prime targets since they represented to them the most invidious and un-Christian aspect of the Egyptians' religion. Accordingly, they systematically destroyed many of the Apis Bulls' tombs and left a trail of havoc through the *Serapeum* (the underground galleries in which the bulls were buried), unaware that their own new religion was distantly rooted in the culture they sought to destroy.

In a sense iconoclasm of this kind is a tacit admission of the great power which the past always wields over the present, and the case of Egypt was no exception. Christians and Copts and Moslems during the first thousand years A.D. all felt the presence of pharaonic Egypt behind them. They could hardly have failed to do so, since wherever they looked there were gigantic monuments, monoliths, pyramids, statues, temples and tombs in various stages of distintegration whose very ruins somehow became more – rather than less – grand as time went on.

Eventually, in the medieval period, the mummy itself began to create a particular interest, although it took perhaps until the sixteenth century before this interest was well-established in Europe. The more the splendours of ancient Egypt receded into the past, the more mysterious they became. The pharaohs and the upper classes of Egypt had had an easy understanding of the complicated array of gods and conflicting theologies. But once the way to explain and resolve those conflicts had been forgotten all that remained were the names of the gods themselves, balefully contending with each other for the worship and service they had once been given. The mummy, whose preparation and purpose had formed an expression of the Egyptians' central religious belief in an after-life, took on for later cultures a kind of magical significance. After the rather literal and pedestrian accounts of the belief had faded from everyday memory, and the legends and tales had been forgotten, what was left seemed to a mystified people a thousand years later to be proof that those ancients really had walked and talked with gods and had been party to the most awesome secrets of the universe.

One of the results of this was that early physicians ground mummies into a powder which they used as medicine. There is a record of an Arab doctor named el Magar prescribing mummy to his patients as early as the twelfth century and by about the end of the sixteenth century mummy had become one of the standard drugs in apothecaries' shops throughout Europe, much prescribed for bruises and wounds though not, oddly enough, for longevity. So popular did mummy become, in fact, that a thriving trade was established with Egypt, and the suppliers had to go to great lengths to keep their stocks of bodies replenished. Tombs were ransacked and the mummies broken up for sale. Tomb-robbery had now taken on a new meaning since the quest was primarily for bodies. When in 1549 the

Glazed composition <u>shabti</u> in its coffin. From the tomb of Amenmes

chaplain to Catherine de Medici, André Thevet, visited Egypt
he joined with two Venetian doctors in breaking into tombs at
Saqqara. Curiously, the demand in France for mummy was
perhaps greater than anywhere else in Europe. Francis I was
said to have carried a little packet of mummy mixed with pul-
verized rhubarb wherever he went in case he fell or was injured.

As supplies of easily-accessible mummies dwindled and the

Turkish authorities occupying Egypt forbade removing them from their tombs, it became necessary to manufacture them to meet the demand. It is possible that this fabrication of mummies had begun as early as 1100–1300, and it rapidly turned into an organized industry run chiefly by Jews. Guy de la Fontaine, the King of Navarre's physician, visited Alexandria in 1564 and inspected a mummy-trader's stocks. The trader, when closely questioned, admitted that none of the bodies was more than four years old. They turned out to be mostly the corpses of beggars, old people – quite often repulsively diseased and raddled – executed criminals and suchlike. The bodies had been 'mummified' by the simple sand-burial technique such as had been used by the poorest Egyptians since pre-dynastic times. In 1660 Vincent le Blanc of Marseilles described the process:

> 'Tis whence [Egypt] the greatest part of Mummy, or flesh buried and rosted [sic] in the sand is gotten, which the wind uncovering, the next passenger brings to town for sale, it being very medicinable. Here you see a dead man is often more serviceable to the living, than the living themselves: yet some approve not of the physick.'

Otherwise, the bodies' abdomens were packed with bitumen, their limbs stuffed with it, the entire corpse bound up tightly and exposed to the heat of the sun.

Opinion was divided as to how efficacious mummy was. Great men like Francis Bacon (1561–1626) claimed that

> 'Mummy hath great force in staunching blood; which, as it may be ascribed to the mixture of balmes that are glutinous, so it may also partake of a secret propriety, in that the blood draweth man's flesh.'

But there were those who remained sceptical. 'This wicked kind of drugge,' wrote Ambrose Paré in 1634, 'doth nothing help the diseased'.

In any case, no one paid any attention. Mummy remained as popular as it had been in 1200 when Abd el Latif wrote that he saw 'momia' taken from the skulls and stomachs of mummies on sale. He himself 'bought three heads filled with it for half a dirham. It differs little from mineral pitch, in place of which it could be used.' In view of this it is strange that the few references to mummies in Shakespeare should have reflected the idea that mummies were noted for their softness and suppleness. Could they have read him, the ancient embalmers would no doubt have been delighted.

Falstaff:

'I had been drown'd, but that the shore was
shelvy and shallow; a death that I abhor;
for the water swells a man; and what a thing
should I have been when I had swell'd! I
should have been a mountain of mummy.'

(*The Merry Wives of Windsor*, Act 3 Scene 5)

Perhaps increasing doubt about the effectiveness of mummy-powder as medicine helped to kill off the trade, but there seems to have been a much more direct economic reason. Reportedly, one of the Jewish mummy-traders had a Christian slave whom he treated abominably and the slave was finally driven to informing on his master. He went to the Pasha at Damietta (near Port Said) and told him about the Jew's lucrative profession. The Pasha promptly threw the trader into prison and released him only in exchange for three hundred pieces of gold. This was obviously such an efficient way of extorting money that the idea caught on, and all the Jewish mummy-traders were rounded up and flung into prison until they bought their own release. It was principally this ingenious 'tax' system which caused the trade to languish. But it never died out completely. Even in the nineteenth century the Arabs were still using mummy-powder mixed with butter as medicine; while, as Harris and Weeks note surprisingly in their book *X-Raying the Pharaohs*,

'Even today there is a regular, though admittedly not very heavy, demand at a New York pharmacy catering to witches for genuine powdered Egyptian mummy. The cost is forty dollars an ounce.'

By the turn of the nineteenth century the somewhat superstitious attraction which Egypt had for Europe was showing signs of becoming more scholarly. The brilliant young Frenchman Jean François Champollion (1790–1832), in producing a partial but correct translation of the hieroglyphic section of the Rosetta Stone, became the first real decipherer of hieroglyphs.

Tourism in Egypt had begun with the ancient Greeks and had been in full swing when Herodotus paid his visit. Those tourists, like today's, left their names and thoughts scribbled about all over the tombs and monuments. Indeed, ancient Egyptian tourists' graffiti often disfigured – and neglect certainly destroyed – so many monuments that one of Ramesses II's sons, Khaemwese, spent much of his time trying to restore them. He seems to have been a withdrawn, melancholy person, liking nothing better than to wander for hours round the Memphis necropolis reading the inscriptions on the tombs and temple walls. When he visited Wenis's pyramid – 5th Dynasty and even then a thousand years old – he carved his own inscription which was not discovered until the French archaeologist J.-P. Lauer found it in 1937, some three thousand years later.

His Majesty has ordered it to be proclaimed that it was the Chief of the craftsmen, the Sem-priest, Prince Khaemwese, who inscribed the name of the King of Upper and Lower Egypt, Wenis, since it was not found on the face of his pyramid, because the Sem-priest Prince Khaemwese much loved to restore the monuments of kings of Upper and Lower Egypt which had fallen into ruin.

By present-day standards of archaeology the 'explorations' of Europeans like Belzoni (born in 1778) were horribly unscientific and they must have damaged irrevocably much that might have yielded important information to a later generation. But the early 'explorers' did have a vivid curiosity combined with a comparative lack of superstitious awe which was a legacy of the era in which they lived. The Age of Reason had given way to the Industrial Revolution in Europe, and it was for men like Belzoni to be intrepid and enquiring.

Belzoni himself visited the Theban necropolis and explored some of the vast underground network of caverns and burial chambers. His account is best quoted in full:

A traveller is generally satisfied when he has seen the large hall, the gallery, the staircase, and as far as he can conveniently go: besides, he is taken up with the strange works he observes cut in various places, and painted on each side of the walls; so that when he comes to a narrow and difficult passage, or to have to descend to the bottom of a well or cavity, he declines taking such trouble, naturally supposing that he cannot see in those classes any thing so magnificent as what he sees above, and consequently deeming it useless to proceed any farther. Of some of these tombs many persons could not withstand the suffocating air, which often causes fainting. A vast quantity of dust rises, so fine that it enters the throat and nostrils, and chokes the nose and mouth to such a degree that it requires great power of lungs to resist it, and the strong effluvia of the mummies. This is not all; the entry, or passage where the bodies are, is roughly cut in the rocks, and the falling of the sand from the upper part or ceiling of the passage causes it to be nearly filled up. In some places there is not more than a vacancy of a foot left, which you must contrive to pass through in a creeping posture like a snail, on pointed and keen stones, that cut like glass. After getting through those passages, some of them two or three thousand yards long, you generally find a more commodious place, perhaps high enough to sit. But what a place of rest! surrounded by bodies, by heaps of mummies in all directions, which, previous to my being accustomed to the sight, impressed me with horror. The blackness of the wall, the faint light given by the candles or torches for want of air, the different objects that surrounded me, seeming to converse with each other, and the Arabs with the candles or torches in their hands, naked and covered with dust, themselves resembling living mummies, absolutely formed a scene that cannot be described. In such a situation I found myself several times, and often returned exhausted and fainting, till at last I became inured to it, and indifferent to what I suffered, except from the dust, which never failed to choke my throat and nose; and though, fortunately, I am destitute of the sense of smelling, I could taste that the mummies were rather unpleasant to swallow. After the exertion of entering into such a place, through a passage of fifty, a hundred, three hundred, or, perhaps six hundred yards, nearly overcome, I sought a resting place, found one, and contrived to sit; but, when my weight bore on the body of an Egyptian, it crushed it like a band-box. I naturally had recourse to my hands to sustain my weight, but they found no better support; so that I sunk altogether among the broken mummies, with a crash of bones, rags, and wooden cases, which raised such a dust as kept me motionless for a quarter of an hour, waiting till it subsided again. I could not remove from the place, however, without increasing it, and every step I took I crushed a mummy in some part or other. Once I was conducted from such a place to another resembling it, through a passage of about twenty feet in length, and no wider than that a body could be forced through. It was choked with mummies, and I could not pass without putting my face in contact with that of some decayed Egyptian; but as the passage inclined downwards, my own weight helped me on; however, I could not avoid being covered with bones, legs, arms, and heads rolling from above. Thus I proceeded from one cave to another, all full of mummies piled up in various ways, some standing, some lying, and some on their heads.

(G. Belzoni, *Narrative of the Operations and Recent Discoveries within the Pyramids, Temples, Tombs and Excavations in Egypt and Nubia.*)

The Englishman, Captain Light, likewise explored part of the same burial complex, no less in a spirit of amazement and adventure. Obviously, side by side with increasingly scholarly interest in Egypt on the part of Europe, an era of notable English eccentrics was beginning to dawn.

Captain Light crept into one of the mummy pits or caverns, which were the common burial places of the ancient Thebans. As it happened to be newly discovered, he found thousands of dead bodies, placed in horizontal layers side by side; these he conceives to be the mummies of the lower order of people, as they were covered only with simple teguments, and smeared over with a composition that preserved the muscles from corruption. "The suffocating smell," he says, "and the natural horror excited by being left alone unarmed with the wild villagers in this charnel house, made me content myself with visiting two or three chambers, and quickly return to the open air." (*The Quarterly Review* no. 37.)

With the more-detailed decipherment of hieroglyphs came a growing interest in the texts which the ancient Egyptians had left behind them on monuments, tomb walls and papyri. Now that the major part of the code had been broken people badly wanted to know what the original texts had said. As more passages were translated and variously revealed themselves as banal or inscrutable, depending on how fragmentary they were and on how many of the words had yet been assigned meanings, a curious desire began to manifest itself in unscientific quarters. This was deliberately to misunderstand, to obscure or to mystify the texts. It can only have arisen from the historically established longing to believe that the Egyptians had in some way been in touch with a long-lost source of wisdom which might yet be recaptured for mankind by some gigantic act of empathy. The embarrassing howlers of pseudo-scholarship to which this led still persist today. Certainly, an early casualty of the battle between reason and the wish for revelation was Joseph Smith, the founder of the Mormon sect in America.

Joseph Smith had evidently acquired three incomplete papyri in the early nineteenth century, and became convinced that one of them was the reportedly lost 'Book of Abraham'. Accordingly, the founder of the Church of Jesus Christ of Latter Day Saints issued his own translation of the papyrus which – while the Mormon Church has not accepted it as scripture on a level with other of Joseph Smith's revelations – has achieved a permanent place perhaps somewhat akin to that of the Apocrypha in the King James version of the Bible.

In the 'Revelations' given to Smith entitled *Doctrine and Covenants: Pearl of Great Price* he announces: 'The Book of Abraham, Translated from the Papyrus, by Joseph Smith. A Translation of some ancient Records, that have fallen into our hands from the catacombs of Egypt. . . . The writings of Abraham while he was in Egypt, called the Book of Abraham, written by his own hand, upon papyrus.' The translation stretches to five chapters. Unfortunately, the Associate Professor of Egyptology at the University of Chicago, Klaus Baer, has recently shown (in the Mormon journal *Dialogue*) that rather than being in Abraham's own handwriting the papyrus dates from about the time of Christ and is in late Ptolemaic or early Roman Period calligraphy. Furthermore, the so-called *Book of Abraham* turns out merely to be a copy of the *Book of Breathings* (see Chapter 4), which was largely compiled from the *Book of the Dead* and which it sometimes replaced during the Roman Period. Hence, far from being a revelation of the Word of God, Smith's papyrus was in fact a rather late specimen of a decidedly heathen collection of magical spells, a discovery which must have left Mormon theologians with a certain amount of deft explaining to do.

It is apparently a long step from an honest self-deception of this kind to the extraordinarily pervasive belief in curses, hauntings and other paranormal phenomena with which people have endowed the mummy itself. And yet behind both can be detected a wish to believe – admittedly in the latter case a wish complicated by a strong and culturally induced feeling that it is wrong to disturb the bodies of the dead. This belief is very clearly expressed by an account dating from 1699 by a Frenchman named Louis Penicher. He wrote a book entitled *Traité des embaumements selon les Anciens et les modernes* in which the following tale occurs:

A Polish traveller bought two mummies in Alexandria, one male and the other female, to ship back to Europe. He divided the bodies into six parts and put each part into a box made of dried tree bark. Into a seventh box the Pole put the amulets from the bodies. At this time the Turks governing Egypt as part of the Ottoman Empire were trying to stop the sale and transport of mummies, thinking that it was some obscure Christian plot to cause mischief. The Pole was forced to bribe with money and wine a Jew, whose job it was to inspect the cargoes of all outgoing ships, telling him that in any case the boxes contained only shellfish.

Then, just before the ship sailed, a priest bound for Jerusalem came aboard. Once at sea he began his customary prayers, but almost immediately a great storm blew up and he was additionally harassed by the vision of two spectres. The crew promptly put this down to the dismembered mummies stowed below in their bark boxes, but the Pole resolutely refused to believe such nonsense until the priest again said his breviary and a second storm arose. The ghosts appeared once more: two figures of a man and a woman dressed as the mummies had been. This time the Pole was convinced and went to the Captain to ask if he could go down into the hold, bring up the boxes and throw them overboard.

The Captain refused, pointing out that it would be lunacy to open the hatches with such a sea running.

When the storm finally died the Pole did go down and throw the boxes overboard, whereupon the Captain cursed him roundly for ever having allowed him to sail with them when it was clear that 'the sea disliked them'. However, the Pole pointed out that Cretan theologians said it was perfectly in order for Christians to transport mummies to cater for the sick, and that the Church defended the practice.

As we have seen in the chapter on tomb robbers there are occasional instances of curses appearing in an Egyptian tomb, or outside on the façade as in the case of the 6th Dynasty mastaba of Khentika Ikhekhi at Saqqara. This inscription reads:

> As for all men who shall enter this my tomb of the necropolis being impure, having eaten those abominations which good spirits which have journeyed to the West abominate . . . there will be judgement with them concerning it in that Western desert in the Council of the Great God . . . an end shall be made for him concerning it in respect of that evil . . . Further, I shall seize his neck like a bird . . . further, I shall cast the fear of myself into him . . .

More specific than Khentika, Ankhtifi in his 9th–10th Dynasty tomb at Moalla inveighed against '. . . any ruler who shall rule in Moalla and shall do evil and wickedness to this coffin (?) and to all stone fitments (?) of this tomb . . . may Hemen [a local god] not accept any of the goods (he offers) and may his heir not inherit.'

But this curse is little more than an edged plea that his *ka*-priests do their job properly and protect his tomb for eternity, whereas the first is concerned more with theological nicety. Neither one has the force of a full-blooded curse levelled specifically at somebody disturbing the mummy itself – perhaps because it was too unthinkable (and even dangerous) to put such an idea into writing. In any case the Penicher story pre-dates the decipherment of hieroglyphics by well over a century, and it is practically certain that no story of a 'cursed' mummy has ever had any foundation in textual fact.

The most famous of all 'curse' stories – and the best instance of a complete fabrication – is the so-called 'Curse of the Mummy's Tomb' which attached itself to the Tutankhamun discovery. It was only forty-one years after the finding of the Deir el Bahri cache and the public's appetite had been periodically whetted by fresh finds, much aided by the coverage of the press. There were already 'mummy' stories in circulation such as those told about two Egyptologists, Professor Brian Emery and Arthur Mace. They are stories which bear a curious resemblance to each other.

According to one story Professor Emery, who in his early days did a good deal of work on Late Period burials, used to lay the mummies he found on trestle tables overnight for closer study the next day. He himself slept in a tent pitched, in true British explorer fashion, among the tables. One night he was reading by lamplight before turning in when he heard a noise outside. Suddenly, a withered mummy-hand appeared round the corner of his tent-flap, grasped the flap and slowly drew it open. Silence. Professor Emery watched as if frozen. When nothing else happened he cautiously went outside and immediately the cause was revealed. One of the trestles on the nearest table had collapsed, letting its burden slide slowly downwards. As it did so the mummy's hand had become caught in the tent flap and had dragged it open.

The story concerning Arthur Mace was vouched for by Margaret Murray, the Egyptologist and anthropologist. Mace used to store his mummies on shelves round his workroom and – again with exemplary *sang-froid* – sleep on a camp bed on the floor. One night he was awoken by a light touch and found that one ill-wrapped arm of a mummy had slipped off the shelf and hung, dangling, with fingers brushing his throat.

Whether or not these stories were true hardly matters. What

is important is that despite the severely rational explanation for both events a public expectation was already set up – an expectation which ensured that, in the mind of the popular press at least, mummies were inevitably surrounded by a delicious horror. This was much compounded by 'The Unlucky Mummy' story which *The Sunday Times* endeavoured finally to lay to rest in 1934. Sir Wallis Budge, the leading expert on the mummy, denied the stories that had begun to circulate and stated that they rested on a series of misunderstandings by a Mr. Douglas Murray and a Mr. T. W. Stead. *The Sunday Times* took up the story.

> These gentlemen said they were acquainted with a mummy which had been brought to England by a lady, and deposited in her drawing-room. The following morning every object breakable in the room was smashed to pieces. On the mummy being removed to an upper room, the same thing happened. Being removed once more to the top floor and locked up in a cupboard by the irate husband, troops of beings breaking crockery and carrying heavy pieces of iron stamped up and down stairs all night, flourishing lights and shaking the staircase to such purpose that all the servants resigned in a body the next day.
>
> About this time a gentleman named Mr. Wheeler presented to the Museum a very handsome inner cover of a great lady who was a Priestess of Amen, and was a member of the College of Amen-Ra at Thebes. This valuable object was accepted by the Trustees, and was placed in a good position for inspection in the First Egyptian Room, where it remained until the year 1920.
>
> ### A SEANCE
>
> Mr. Douglas Murray and Mr. Stead came, and, with other people, examined this interesting object, and they decided that the expression on the face was that of a living soul in torment, and they wished to hold a seance in the room and to perform certain experiments with the object of remov-

ing the anguish and misery from the eyes of the coffin-lid. The story of their views, which they published in the papers, had the effect of making people remember the mummy which smashed the crockery and furniture in the lady's drawing-room, and so, little by little, the coffin-lid in the British Museum became the hero of a whole set of stories. People wrote from far New Zealand, sending money, and asking that lilies might be laid at the foot of the case containing the coffin. A gentleman from Algiers also sent money for floral offerings to be placed before it. Ladies in England did the same. Sad to say, I believe that the money offerings were absorbed by the hard-hearted Treasurer of the Museum, and no flowers were bought.

NEW LIFE

Later, the story gained new life, but the treatment took on an entirely new application. According to this, so many complaints were received by the Trustees as to the dire things that were done in the Egyptian Rooms, that they at length ordered the cover to be removed to the basement. The story then went on to say that the staff at the British Museum were terrified because several had been smitten with death and disease owing to this cover. It was further said that I had been privately instructed to negotiate the sale of this terrible object to a wealthy American. Still according to the story, this American took the object on the *Titanic*, and the cover made the *Titanic* smite the iceberg. But its owner, being a man of wealth, bribed right and left, and succeeded in having the cover removed to safety.

On arrival in America, the lid continued to work calamities and spread diseases amongst everyone with whom it came into contact, and at length the enterprising American sold it to a Canadian, who took it to Montreal. Even there it continued its evil course, and when finally its owner decided to send it back to England, it sunk when the *Empress of Ireland* went down in the St. Lawrence River, where, let us hope, it still rests.

Inner coffin cover of a Priestess of Amun. It has been surrounded by superstititions and stories, including the claim that it was on board the TITANIC when it sank.

THE FACTS

Now let us come back to facts. The British Museum never possessed either mummy or coffin or cover which did such things. The Trustees never gave any order for the removal of the cover to the basement, although during the air-raids it was put in a place of safety.

The Trustees have no power to sell any object under their charge, and even to sell duplicates they have to obtain a special Act of Parliament; still less has any Keeper, such as myself, any authority to dispose of anything under any circumstances, whether by gift or sale.

I did not sell the cover to an American. The cover never went on the *Titanic*. It never went to America. It was not sold to anybody in Canada, and it is still in the First Egyptian Room in the British Museum, bearing the number 22542.

No. 22542, now in the Second Egyptian Room, is the jacket illustration of this book (also see opposite page).

By 1922, when Howard Carter discovered Tutankhamun, the public's imagination was only too suggestible. When Lord Carnarvon (Carter's sponsor) died suddenly following a mosquito bite in April 1923, the news provided the momentum for what was to be an almost endless series of newspaper stories about the 'Curse of Tut' which would infallibly strike down all who had been associated with breaking his long sleep. In point of fact the whole thing can be dated quite precisely to a letter written by Marie Corelli to the *New York World* a fortnight before Carnarvon died. Marie Corelli was a popular romantic novelist of the time and in this letter she excelled herself in striking exactly the right note of concerned foreboding which would guarantee the survival of what was unwittingly her greatest-ever plot. Part of her letter read:

> I cannot but think some risks are run by breaking into the last rest of a King of Egypt whose tomb is specially and solemnly guarded, and robbing him of his possessions.

195

According to a rare book I possess, which is not in the British Museum, entitled "The Egyptian History of the Pyramids" . . . the most dire punishment follows any rash intruder into a sealed tomb.

This book gives long and elaborate lists of the treasures buried with several of the kings, and among these are named "divers secret poisons enclosed in boxes in such wise that they who touch them shall not know how they come to suffer".

When Carnarvon died with commendable promptness two weeks later, the press had a field-day, aided and abetted by another, even more successful, novelist – Sir Arthur Conan Doyle, the creator of Sherlock Holmes. With the assurance of one whose brain was internationally renowned for the solution of his own mysteries, he gave his opinion that Carnarvon's death might have been caused by 'elementals – not souls, not spirits – created by Tutankhamun's priests to guard the tomb'.

This endorsement gave the 'curse' legend all the impetus it needed. In 1926 Arthur Weigall, who had been Inspector-General of Antiquities to the Egyptian Government, was interviewed by *The Morning Post* following the death of a French Egyptologist named Bénédite of the Louvre in Paris who had been involved in the Tutankhamun researches and had just died from a stroke brought on by the heat in the Valley of the Kings. *The Morning Post* quoted Weigall as saying: 'While I cannot exactly say that I subscribe in believing in the efficacy of such curses, I must admit that some very strange things – call them coincidences if you will – have happened in connection with the Luxor excavations.' He then added gratuitously that six weeks before Carnarvon's death he had watched the Earl joking and laughing before going into Tutankhamun's tomb and had told a writer standing nearby that he 'gave him six weeks to live'. Needless to say, when Weigall himself died in 1934 many agreed that he was another victim of the curse.

Thereafter occurred a series of some twenty deaths which

were ascribed to the 'curse', some of the alleged victims having had only the thinnest possible connection with the opening of the Luxor tomb. It would be momentarily diverting to invent a curse retrospectively to apply to any discovery – plutonium, perhaps, or North Sea Gas – and try to build up a case from the fatalities associated with it (no matter how tenuously) to show that there was indeed a malediction operating. It is a safe maxim that if there is enough will to believe in something, evidence will soon be found to corroborate it. In the case of the 'Curse of Tut' the bulk of Egyptologists and scholars poured scorn on the myth from the outset. Sir Wallis Budge, an authority on hieroglyphs, staked his reputation on saying that in none of the texts inside Tutankhamun's tomb was there an inscription which read: 'Death shall come on swift wings to him that toucheth the tomb of a Pharaoh'. This 'text' was either an inspired mistranslation (like that of the *Book of Abraham*) or a downright fabrication. Nevertheless, it appeared time and time again in newspaper after newspaper.

If ever the myth of the curse showed signs of flagging, the odd renegade scholar could always be relied on to pop up with a reedy dissenting voice which was inevitably more melodramatic and therefore excited greater public attention than the chill tones of flat denial.

'I am absolutely certain,' said Dr. Mardras, a translator of papyri, 'that the Egyptians during a period of 7,000 years knew how to condense round their mummies a dynamism by means of magic ritual, and amulets charged with fluids of which we have only the vaguest idea today.' He did not explain how, if such a 'dynamism' had been remotely effective, the long history of mummies happened also to be the long history of tomb robbery.

By 1934 the whole story had such a grip on the public's imagination that the Curator of the Egyptology Department of the Metropolitan Museum in New York decided to carry out a census. He found that out of the twenty-six people who had been present at the opening of Tutankhamun's burial chamber, six had died within ten years. Of twenty-two people who had witnessed the opening of the sarcophagus, only two had died. And of ten who – most dangerously, it would have seemed – had been present at the unwrapping of Tutankhamun's mummy, every one was still alive.

Howard Carter himself said unequivocally that 'sane people should dismiss such inventions with contempt'. His contempt was evidently proof against the curse, since the 'swift wings' took until 1939 to catch up with him. Many of his colleagues intimately involved in the Luxor dig lived well into the Second World War. Several were still alive afterwards, including Sir Alan Gardiner, who in 1949 was seventy, and Dr. Derry (he had performed the autopsy on the mummy), who was seventy-four. Lady Beauchamp (née Herbert: she was Lord Carnarvon's daughter) was present at the opening of the tomb and at the British Museum's Tutankhamun Exhibition in 1972, still very much alive and in her eighties.

Also very much alive and just entering its fifties was the 'curse' itself, trotted out by the *Daily Telegraph* (among others) on 5 February 1972 to explain the death of the Egyptian official responsible for shipping the treasures to Britain. One would have thought by now the 'curse' would have been laid to rest. Yet one or two 'unexplained' oddities are still cited from time to time as proof of people's reluctance to part with their cherished superstitions.

The strange thing is that anyone should ever have wished to put curses into the mouth of that boy-pharaoh. Given the presumed circumstances of his death, it seems more likely that the priests buried him with the most perfunctory and standard selection of texts from the *Book of the Dead*. And if he had been to some extent disgraced then the thought of his body being disturbed at some future date might not have concerned them unduly. In any case there is so much to marvel at in his singular discovery that there is no need for the addition of extra awe. The pity and splendour of the feather fan which Sir Alan Gardiner saw brought out into daylight after three thousand years far exceeds any *frisson* the popular press could induce.

Meanwhile, away from the realms of fanciful speculation, a good deal of serious work has been done on mummies. Much of it has been of the kind more usually found in the forensic laboratories of a police force since the motive may be the same in each case: to discover as much as possible about an un-identified body which might lead to its identification. If the identity is already known, most bodies will in any case yield information about the person's circumstances while living and the manner of his death.

The scientific examination of Egyptian mummies properly dates back to the work done by Gaston Maspero in 1889 and G. E. Smith in 1912 on the mummies from the two Theban caches. They did not learn a great deal, chiefly for two reasons. First – something which reflects highly on their sense of responsibility as archaeologists – they were unwilling to unwrap many of the bodies because they had been so beautifully ban-daged. Second, they had practically no access to X-ray equip-ment. Roentgen's development of X-rays since 1895 had been impressive, but his apparatus was too unwieldy and cumber-some for easy transport. Nevertheless, Smith did manage to X-ray the mummy of Tuthmosis IV.

In fact it was not until December 1966 that the first systematic X-raying of mummies, using modern equipment, began. The team of which James E. Harris and Kent Weeks were members had gone to Cairo on the premise that it was the mummies' teeth which, above all, could in nearly every case provide useful information since the teeth were generally the part of the human body which were least susceptible to decay after death. Among other things the team hoped to establish that it would be possible to distinguish between the social classes by referring to dentition, assuming that the lower the class from which the person had come the coarser his diet would have been and hence the worse the condition of his teeth.

They expected to find evidence of disease, for as early as 1907–8 Elliot Smith and Wood Jones had established that the skulls of ancient Egyptians in the Nile Valley showed evidence of every dental abnormality known nowadays, whether or not caused by disease. However, since sugar cane and refined sugar were not introduced until after the Arab conquest in A.D. 641, it was clearly not this which had caused decay. It is true that the Egyptians had used honey extensively as their only source of sweetness, but it does not produce dental caries on anything like the scale of refined white sugar. Indeed, 'holes' or cavities are not very often found in the ancient Egyptians' teeth, this being much more the disease of the modern West (although now spreading throughout the world with the easy availability of sugar).

What the Egyptians did suffer from was dental attrition: that is, the surface of the tooth showed great wear, often being worn down to a stub level with the gum. This gave rise to what must have been one of the most common and painful of the Egyptians' diseases: dental abscesses. These were of two kinds. When the surface enamel of the tooth was worn away the inner pulp and its nerve were exposed and must frequently have become infected. Secondly, because this attrition caused unequal pressures on the chewing surfaces of the teeth, stress was set up in the tissues surrounding the remaining teeth and inflammation set in there as well. So the Egyptians were prone to abscesses of the root of the tooth and abscesses of the surrounding gum. Clearly many of them must have died (as they had no doubt lived) in excruciating pain from dental abscesses which had led to generalized septicaemia and in some cases to meningitis.

What caused this excessive wear of their teeth? A clue may be found in the nickname certain Greek writers gave the Egyptians, as Sir A. Ruffer in his book *Food in Egypt* (1919) explains:

The most important food of the Egyptians was bread made of various cereals, wheat, barley, and possibly as well from lotus seeds and dum-palm dates. The fondness of Egyptians for bread was so well known that they were nicknamed 'artophagoi', or 'eaters of bread'; it was the food *par excellence*, and the word was and has remained synonymous with food in this country. The most terrible curse was 'They shall hunger without bread and their bodies die.' . . . Bread and oil formed the main food for the people. The troops and the king's messengers were given 20 deben (about 4 lbs) of bread daily as rations, which was carried by numerous parties accompanying the march.

Obviously, a food which formed the major part of the Egyptians' diet was most likely to be responsible for the condition of their teeth. But why should it have caused such wear, and what other evidence is available?

Luckily, we have the wall-paintings inside tombs as well as the little models of servants at their various kinds of work to provide the information. Thanks to the hundreds of illustrations and models we know exactly how the Egyptians baked their bread, and at once it becomes possible to see that during the different stages – from reaping the corn with a flint-toothed sickle to baking it in brick ovens – the bread could have become contaminated with a great deal of grit, sand, and mud-brick dust. Reasoning that if there had been appreciable quantities of grit it could easily account for the abnormal wear of their teeth, a dentist named Filce Leek set out to analyse samples of Egyptian bread which had been found in tombs of different periods. The analyses did indeed reveal that the bread contained easily-measurable quantities of sand, mica, bits of rock, quartz, brick and assorted dust and grit. In fact, the Egyptians' daily bread acted like sandpaper on their teeth and, as Filce Leek himself pointed out in his published results, *Teeth and Bread in Ancient Egypt*: 'There is no difficulty in believing the story written in the Talmud . . . that one of Joseph's fellow prisoners was the Pharaoh's chief baker, and that the cause of his incarceration and the subsequent loss of his head was the royal displeasure with gritty bread.' Since bread was a staple part of the diet of rich and poor alike, it has unfortunately been impossible to define any real relationship between dentition and class. Nevertheless, the teeth-patterns themselves have revealed one surprising fact, which is that the pharaohs were a very mixed bunch whose familiar relationships were often impossible to guess. Far from the clear royal line in which a particular physical characteristic is traceable from one generation to the next (as in the Amenophis/Akhenaten/Smenkhkare/Tutankhamun line) there seems to have been a surprising lack of royal continuity at certain times. As Harris and Weeks point out, if the different mummies had been found in different parts of the world 'no one would have assumed any relationship between them'.

The actual cause of death can rarely be deduced from the scientific examination of a mummy since most fatal diseases leave no mark on the bones, and the tissues are too withered or impregnated with natron to make the presence of germs or virus cells detectable. There are nonetheless several instances where a disease has been evident at the time of death, such as acute dental abscess or a fulminating attack of smallpox. Unfortunately it has so far proved impossible to determine whether certain wounds, such as bone fractures, occurred before or after death. If such a technique ever is invented, the question of the hole in Tutankhamun's skull will perhaps be satisfactorily answered. Meanwhile, a certain amount can be deduced from the battle-wounds on several mummies.

It was obviously impossible to embalm properly or immediately anyone who died away from a town – on a battlefield, for instance. From papyri it seems that the 17th Dynasty King Seqenenre died in battle, and his alleged mummy certainly seems to confirm this. He is in bad shape and must have been in an advanced state of decomposition before the embalmers began their work, so presumably it had taken them some little time to retrieve his body. A large hole has been smashed through his skull on one side; and although it is quite consistent with a battle-wound and would tend to confirm the papyri still further, it is also possible that it was made after death – maybe even centuries later by tomb-robbers. Consequently we still cannot be certain that the body we think of as Seqenenre's is really his. On the other hand much more can be deduced from several hastily-wrapped bodies which have become known as the Mentuhotep archers. These, quite clearly killed in battle, were merely bandaged and lain together in a cache. Their viscera were not removed, and from the condition of the bodies it seems that some time must have elapsed between their deaths and their burial. Many of the bodies bear wounds which have been definitely attributed to vulture-beaks. But it is the arrow-wounds which provide the greatest interest. From the heads and broken-off shafts still lodged inside the bodies it has been possible to calculate the angle from which the archers were shot. It turns out that they were all shot from above, which has provided valuable evidence about the battle itself. (For greater detail see H. E. Winlock, *The Slain Soldiers of Nebhepetre Mentuhotpe* – New York, 1945, which has excellent illustrations of the vulture damage.)

By and large it has been possible to make the following generalizations from close examination of Egyptian mummies:

(i) The Egyptians were mostly quite short, averaging between 5ft. 2in. and 5ft. 4in. although Ramesses II was six feet tall.

(ii) They never wore restrictive footwear – only sandals or nothing – since there is no evidence of non-inherited foot deformity.

(iii) There was a considerable incidence of children's diseases.

(iv) Their life expectancy was low: forty would have been considered a good age; yet Ramesses II lived to be ninety, Pepy II to a hundred, while the Westcar Papyrus gives Djedi's age as a hundred and ten.

(v) Since there was so much grit in the food dental attrition was rife and hence acute toothache must have been endemic.

(vi) Spinal arthritis was common and might have been caused by primary infections such as brucellosis and typhoid.

(vii) Among the diseases unknown in ancient Egypt were tuberculosis, syphilis, leprosy and rickets (a deficiency disease, here ruled out by the sunshine and by the vitamins in the everyday diet).

Yet another myth which science has disposed of but which still lingers among some laymen is the idea that 'mummy' wheat found in Egyptian tombs can be made to germinate and grow. It is easy to see how attractive this notion is – that living grain could be stored away after the harvest and then taken out after three thousand years to be sown and grown, directly continuing a process begun three millennia earlier. To grow the grain which an ancient Egyptian reaped is a nice idea; so is hatching out a fossilized dinosaur egg. Unfortunately, botanists have long known that the wheat germ dies in a very few years. The chances of germination after a mere twenty-five years are practically nil, and in the 1930's Wilfred Parker, the Director of the National Institute of Agricultural Botany in Cambridge, conducted a careful experiment with some grain supplied by Sir Wallis Budge from a 19th Dynasty tomb in Western Thebes. The results conformed exactly to the predictions. Microscopic examination of the embryos before planting had told Dr. Parker that they were dead, but he planted the seeds anyway. Within sixteen days they had all rotted and a thick growth of mould covered the sand in which he had planted them.

What had occasionally misled people, as Dr. Parker pointed out, was the modern Egyptians' habit of storing their own wheat in the halls of ancient tombs – grain which of course germinated since it was only a year or so old. In a letter to *The Times* in 1934 he wrote:

Perhaps it is too much to hope that this evidence will finally dispose of the myth concerning the growth of seed which has lain for centuries in ancient tombs or temples; but if it serves to deter even a limited number of people from wasting their money and their time (and, incidentally, the time of such institutes as my own) over speculations on or in such seed, the investigation will not have been in vain.

If all hope of growing ancient wheat is as dead as the grain itself the writer likes to speculate on the possibility of grinding it into flour and making bread from it. Are there any biochemical reasons why this shouldn't work? Does more than the germ itself degenerate? Would more yeast than usual be needed? Would it taste musty and stale? A great deal of 'mummy' wheat has been found: it would surely be worth using some of it to bake a loaf, if only for the slightly hysterical pleasure of eating ancient Egyptian bread.

The scientific approach to Egyptology has a distinguished history dating from before the turn of this century. Yet this chapter would not be complete without a sidelong glance at its disreputable counterpart which persists in a grotesque parody of scientific method and which has nothing to do with Egyptology proper. This is the field of pseudo-scholarship whose researchers are widely known to English-speaking Egyptologists as 'pyramidiots'. 'Pyramidiocy' is a disease characterized by obsessive interest in pyramidology, numerology, various other -ologies including astrology and the occult, and it quite frequently overlaps into the downright insane.

It is unfortunate that Egyptology attracts cranks in such numbers, for like all branches of archaeology it needs hard scholarship and not the speculations of the afflicted. Of every relic known to Egyptology the Great Pyramid of Giza has attracted the most interest from such people. That it is only one of over seventy remaining pyramids is apparently neither here nor there, any more than is the fact that it is not the oldest, as we have seen. It simply happens to be the biggest; and for that reason (and that reason alone) it has been the most talked-about, the most investigated, the most often measured and the most incautiously theorized-about artefact of ancient Egypt. The kind of personal service into which this very public monument has been pressed is well exemplified by a book called *The Great Pyramid of Gizeh* (published in London in 1923).

Its author, Francis W. Chapman, was evidently assured that the very word 'pyramid' held a secret. Once convinced of this, he laboured hard to produce all sorts of highly inventive derivations for the word to confirm his theory. The first syllable of his 'original' word 'Pi Ra Mo Id' (which apparently meant 'that great sun-god') set Mr. Chapman off into speculating that the Great Pyramid was somehow a monument to π (the 3·1416 ratio).

Unfortunately for him there is no substitute for scholarship. As we saw in Chapter 4 'pyramid' was not the Egyptians' word for the structure, which was *mr*. The prefix 'm', which is common in Semitic languages, means 'place', while ' 'r' means 'to ascend'. *mr* very probably meant 'place of ascent'. This is analogous to their original word for the tombs we know as *mastabas*: *mihat*, from *mʿhʿt* which meant 'place of standing up' (resurrection?).

Chapman's account of the Great Pyramid's purpose and function is merely one of a continuing stream of theories from people who apparently cannot accept that this extremely impressive building was nothing more than Khufu's idea of a decent tomb. Some of the wilder theories are:

(i) That the Great Pyramid was built as a gigantic horoscope for Khufu: a sort of huge astrological folly.

(ii) That it was built as a house for Osiris.

(iii) That it was built as a landing-mark for flying saucers.

(iv) That the Great Pyramid is 'an allegorical representation in structural form of the Messianic

Prophecies, which the Egyptians perverted and applied to Osiris'. (From *Mystery of the Great Pyramid* by Basil Stewart, London 1929).

This idea has been taken up time and time again and has always led to obsessive numerology. Thus a Colonel J. Garnier, in his book *The Great Pyramid, its Builder and its Prophecy* (London, 1912) wrote that he had measured the Pyramid's Great Gallery in so-called Pyramid Inches and had discovered that the next year (1913) was to be 'the great day of the Lord'. And in case 1913 turned out not to be the dawn of the great Day after all, Col. Garnier hedged his bet by adding a footnote: 'There seems to be some possibility that the date of our Lord's birth may have been two years later than the date generally accepted, in which case the date indicated by the Great Pyramid would be A.D. 1915'.

This theory that the Great Pyramid is a vast stone prophecy found much currency among a sect known as the British Israelites, who appeared to believe that Britain somewhere concealed the Lost Tribe of Israel. Adam Rutherford, in *The Great Pyramid – A Scientific Revelation* (London, 1939), pointed out the significance of the unit of measurement known as the 'Pyramid Inch'.

> The Pyramid's revelation is primarily and specially addressed to the British Race (in the British Empire and U.S.A.) for these are the only people who use the inch. History has proved that the Pyramid's Divine message is addressed in the first instance to the Anglo-Saxon Race for all the Pyramid symbolism at present known to us has been discovered by members of that race. Indeed, it is remarkable that almost all of the eminent Pyramidists have been Scotsmen . . .

It was Adam Rutherford who worked out that one diagonal of the Great Pyramid's base points unerringly to the British Isles; and it was he who calculated the angle of the Great Pyramid's interior passages as being the Messianic Angle of $26° 18' 9.63''$

(using the presumed length of Christ's lifetime, thirty-three and a half years, as the length of the hypotenuse of a right-angled triangle whose base was thirty years – this being the age at which Christ began his ministry).

The Great Pyramid has also been seen as an observatory, and as a huge water-pump. The water-pump theory has been developed by an American named Edward J. Kunkel of Ohio who was so convinced by a working model that in 1961 he took out U.S. Patent no. 2887956 on it. This theory entailed seeing Khufu's huge red granite sarcophagus as an alarm bell which, cradled in baulks of timber and buoyed up by the water-level in the King's Chamber, would bump against the ceiling and emit 'deep mellow tones' as a warning that the water was getting dangerously high.

In case anyone thinks that some of these sources are suspiciously old they need only check with a good library to find that the torrent of literature on pyramidology and related subjects has never slackened. Adam Rutherford has himself written at least four books, the most recent dated 1972. And so it goes on, with books like John Ivimy's *The Sphinx and the Megaliths*, which seeks to show that Stonehenge was really built by migrant Egyptians, and endless nonsense identifying the ancient gods with spacemen. It appears that Jehovah's Witnesses believe Pharaoh (which pharaoh?) to have been a tool of the devil; but it is certainly not the devil who has used – and continues to misuse – the pharaohs and their culture as a convenient way of off-loading the superstitions, myth and claptrap which is the débris of a decaying Western religion.

Such aberrations apart, ancient Egypt still has a justifiable grip on our cultural imagination. Thousands of Europeans walk about wearing little silver *ankhs* round their necks, many of them presumably with no idea of the age and meaning of the symbol. Two of our best-known operas are set in Egypt: Mozart's *Magic Flute* and Verdi's *Aida* – the latter having a libretto based on an original scenario by the French Egyptologist Auguste Mariette. At a somewhat different level there are also horror films about re-vivified mummies much beloved by devotees of the British Hammer Film company. Their inaccuracy of detail is perhaps what gives them their flavour, since the wild, swathed giants plunging through French windows with their stiff gait and casualty-ward bandages are rather more impressive than the reality of small brown men with bad teeth ever could be. Yet such films are inescapably the latest incarnation of the old 'curse of the mummy', a mythology which, as we have seen, dates back at least to the seventeenth century.

So much is now known about the upper-class ancient Egyptians' lives and culture that there is no longer any room for transcendental speculations. If there must be mystery, then it should stem from a recognition that mummies are the bodies of dead people which have survived as ours will assuredly not. They are our most direct link with an extinct civilization whose customs and beliefs, through Greek and Jewish channels, predetermined much of Europe's religion and culture. Many of the origins of our own civilization are directly traceable to ancient Egypt.

In a curious way the survival of the bodies of men, women, children and animals whose lives were extinguished so long ago offers little comfort. Their *ba*s, their *ka*s, their *akhu* and all died with the language that invented them; yet the bodies which they so carefully prepared 'for eternity' provide us now with vivid data about what their lives were like. It is those bodies which annihilate time, and therein lies what mystery there ever could be. Yet we know instinctively that some of the attention we pay to the past is a partial unwillingness to accept the present and an implied plea to the future to take a similar interest in ourselves. It is this perhaps misguided egotism which, lacking nearly all living religious tradition, buries 'Time Capsules' instead of bodies in the hope that one day scholars may translate what we once said and deduce from our artefacts who we once were.

A note on the spelling of names

The spelling of any language that has to be transliterated into the Roman alphabet (which may not have the appropriate sounds) is always a headache. In the case of ancient Egyptian, which like modern Arabic was written in consonants only, the vowels being omitted, the spelling presents particular problems. Furthermore, in the case of names many of them became 'Hellenized' by the Greeks and represent what they thought the Egyptian original sounded like (a good example of this being the corruption of Ramesses II's Egyptian name to Ozymandias).

Readers unfamiliar with the pharaohs' names will undoubtedly be baffled by the apparent lack of standardization in the literature of Egyptology. Here we have aimed to be consistent and in accordance with the latest accepted scholarship. For example, we have always rendered the 18th Dynasty pharaohs as 'Amenophis' rather than 'Amenhotep' or 'Amenhotpe'.

Where Amun is concerned it is spelt thus if it stands alone or with a prefix as in Tutankhamun. But if it is followed by a suffix the vowel changes to 'e' as in Amen-Re.

We spell the sun god as 'Re' although 'Ra' is a perfectly common and acceptable alternative. The Egyptians actually spelt it *r'* leaving it anybody's guess.

The word *shabti* can also be found variously spelt *shawabti* and *ushabti* since the Egyptians themselves eventually forgot the word's derivation. We have opted for the shortest form.

Where the transliteration of modern Arabic is concerned we have aimed for the most accurate rendering of the sound unless, as in the case of a word like *serdab*, the version has already been firmly incorporated into Egyptology.

AKH   A spirit released at death, usually represented in the form of a bird

AMENTIT   Region of the setting sun where the dead were thought to dwell under the rule of *Osiris*

ANUBIS   Jackal-headed god of embalming

APIS   The sacred bull of Memphis, held to be *Ptah*'s earthly manifestation. Apis bulls were buried with great ceremony in underground galleries at Saqqara called the *Serapeum*

APOPHIS   A huge serpent thought to inhabit the seventh region of the underworld and attack the sun-god's boat as it sailed through

ATEN   Form of the sun-god made supreme under Akhenaten

ATUM   The god of the setting sun. Identified with *Re* as the world's creator

BA   The soul or spirit of a man able to leave the mummy and take many forms, but most often represented as a human-headed bird

BASTET   Cat goddess of fertility and festivity

BENBEN   Conical or pyramid-shaped stone associated with the mound on which the sun-god rose from the ocean of chaos. Placed on top of a squat pillar in Old Kingdom sun temples but in the New Kingdom it formed the capstone of an *Obelisk*

BOOK OF THE DEAD   A collection of up to two hundred spells, often illustrated, and written on papyrus which was placed in the tomb to help the deceased reach the other world safely

CANOPIC JARS/CHESTS   A set of four jars, named after the Greek hero Canopus. Their stoppers were usually carved with the heads of the four Sons of *Horus*. They contained the embalmed stomach, liver, lungs and intestines. They were kept in a *Canopic Chest* which had four compartments.

CARTONNAGE   Plaster-stiffened linen, often used as a painting surface

CARTOUCHE   A *Hieroglyphic* symbol representing rope twisted into a bullet shape with a royal name written within it

CENSER   An incense burner, usually in the form of a long metal handle with a bowl at one end

DEMOTIC   Very cursive script which evolved from the *Hieratic* script from about 700 BC onwards. A Greek word meaning 'of the people'. Written on monuments and papyri

DUAT   The underworld. It was divided into twelve regions through which flowed a river. The sun-god sailed along it during the hours of darkness.

EMMER   A form of wheat known to the ancient Egyptians

ENNEAD   Greek word meaning 'a group of nine'. Applied to a group of nine gods in the Great Ennead of Heliopolis or Memphis

GEB   The earth-god in the creation legend of Heliopolis. Male partner of *Nut*. Sometimes called the Father of the Gods

HATHOR   Mother goddess and patroness of love and festivity. Worshipped as a COW or as a woman with cow's ears and horns. Consort of *Horus*

HIERATIC   Cursive script. An adaptation of *Hieroglyphs* to the medium of ink and brush on papyrus. From the Greek word meaning 'priestly writing'. It first occurs at the same time as *Hieroglyphs*.

HIEROGLYPHS   Pictorial script designed for carving or large-scale painting. First appears c.3100 BC. From the Greek word meaning 'sacred writing'

HORUS   Originally a hawk-headed sky-god associated with the sun. The great sphinx at Giza represents another form of *Horus*. Son and avenger of *Osiris*, *Horus* is sometimes represented as a small boy.

IBU   A tent in which the ritual washing and purification of a corpse took place before the embalming process began

IMHOTEP   Architect of the step pyramid at Saqqara. Later deified and identified by the Greeks with Asklepios, their god of healing and medicine

ISIS   Sister and wife of *Osiris* and mother of *Horus*. The foremost mother-goddess of ancient Egypt. She was closely connected with mummification as one of the four female protectors of the dead.

KA   The life-force of a man, born within him as a twin, but not released to have a separate existence until after death when it resided in the *Ka*-statue in the tomb chapel

KOHL   Ground malachite (a green ore of copper) or galena (a black ore of lead), mixed with water and applied as an eye cosmetic

MASTABA   Tomb built on a rectangular ground-plan with slightly sloping walls. The superstructure was originally solid over an underground burial chamber, but later became honeycombed with highly decorated rooms.

MESUT   The Egyptian word for 'evening', literally meaning 'time of birth' as it was thought that the stars were piglets, offspring of a heavenly sow who gave birth to them at the end of each day.

MR   Egyptian word for 'pyramid'. Possibly meaning 'place of ascent'

MUU-DANCERS   Dancers in the funerary rites

NATRON   A salt that occurs naturally in Egypt (sodium carbonate and bicarbonate). Used as a purifying agent and to dry out the body in the mummification process

NAUNET   The female form of *Nun*. One of the four female creative beings in the Hermopolis creation legend

NECROPOLIS   Greek word meaning 'city of the dead'. Used to describe Egyptian cemeteries

NEFERTUM   The god of the lotus. Son of *Ptah* and *Sekhmet*

NEITH   Warrior-goddess. One of the four female protectors of the dead

NEPHTHYS   Sister and wife of *Set* and sister of *Isis*. One of the four female protectors of the dead

NUN   The ocean of chaos from which the creator-god arose to create the world. Also one of the four male creative beings in the Hermopolis creation legend

NUT   The sky-goddess who gave birth to the sun each day. Often represented as a woman bending over the earth, her body spangled with stars

OBELISK   A tapering, four-sided shaft of stone, capped with a *Benben*. Replaced the squat pillar of the Old Kingdom sun temples

OGDOAD   Greek word meaning 'group of eight'. Applied to group of eight gods in the Ogdoad of Hermopolis

OSIRIS   God of the dead. Husband and brother of *Isis* and father by her of *Horus*. Also god of vegetation whose life and death reflected the annual growth of crops. All Egyptians hoped to be identified with him after death and live in his kingdom of *Amentit*.

PAPYRUS   A parchment-like writing material made from the pith of the Cyperus papyrus plant, cut into strips and joined into sheets

PHARAOH   Hebrew word derived from the Egyptian for 'palace'. Title of the king of Egypt

PR-NFR   Literally 'good house'. Another name for the *Wabt* or place of embalming

PTAH   Great creator-god always represented as mummiform human wearing a skull-cap. In the Memphite family he was husband of *Sekhmet* and father of *Nefertum*. The *Apis* bull was his earthly manifestation.

PTAH-SOKARIS-OSIRIS   Composite funerary god, often represented exactly like *Osiris*

PYRAMIDION   Term applied to the capstone of brick-built, pyramid-shaped New Kingdom tomb chapels. Sometimes applied to an *Obelisk*'s capstone (see *Benben*)

RE   The sun-god at his noonday strength. Creator of the world according to the Heliopolis creation legend

RE-HORAKHTY-ATUM   Composite form of the sun-god representing his different aspects. *Re*, god of the noonday sun, *Horakhty* the morning sun and *Atum* the setting sun

RISHI   From the Arabic word meaning 'feather'. Applied to wooden anthropoid coffins decorated with a pattern of feathers during the late Second Intermediate Period

ROSTJAU   Region of the Kingdom of the Dead near the entrance to the underworld. Originally probably part of the necropolis at Saqqara

SAFF   Arabic word for 'row'. Used to describe Middle Kingdom tombs at Thebes where the row of entrances cut into the back wall of a courtyard resembles a row of pillars

SARCOPHAGUS   Stone coffin, either rectangular or human-shaped. The word in Greek means 'flesh-eating' because the Greeks thought certain stone had the property of devouring the corpses put in coffins made from it

SEKHMET   Lioness-headed goddess associated with the destroying heat of the sun. Wife of *Ptah* and mother of *Nefertum*. Patroness of doctors

SERAPEUM   The underground galleries at Saqqara in which *Apis* bulls were buried

SERDAB   Arabic word for 'cellar'. Applied to walled-up room in mastabas which housed the *Ka*-statue. Only an eye-level slit connected it with the offering place in the tomb chapel.

SET   Brother and murderer of *Osiris*. Husband of *Nephthys*. God of the desert, darkness and storms. Represented as an animal with a snout, long ears and a forked tail

SHABTI   A figurine representing the dead person which evolved into a servant carrying agricultural implements. Inscribed with Chapter Six of the *Book of the Dead* (the *shabti* formula) which enabled it to carry out agricultural duties on behalf of its owner in the other world

SHU   God of the air. One of the nine great gods of Heliopolis. Male partner of *Tefnut*

SOKARIS   Hawk-headed funerary god of the Memphis necropolis, associated by the Old Kingdom with *Ptah* and by the Middle Kingdom with *Osiris*

STELA   An inscribed slab of stone often set into another surface

TATENEN   The mound of earth which emerged from *Nun* upon which the creator-god sat to create the world

TEFNUT   Goddess of moisture. One of the nine great gods of Heliopolis. Female partner of *Shu*, sometimes lioness-headed

TEKENU   Ritual object of disputed significance resembling a crouched man in a sack. Dragged on a sled in funeral processions

THOTH   Ibis-headed scribe of the gods. God of the moon and mediator between *Horus* and *Set*

WABT   Literally 'the pure place'. The building, sometimes a temporary structure, in which the process of embalming took place

WAS   Animal-headed staff, ending in two curved prongs

BIBLIOGRAPHY

CHAPTER ONE: The Background

Cerney, Jaroslav. *Ancient Egyptian Religion*. New York: Hillary House, 1957.
*Frankfort, Henri. *Ancient Egyptian Religion*. New York: Columbia University Press, 1948.

CHAPTER TWO: Mummification

Budge, E. A. Wallis. *The Mummy*. New York: Macmillan, 1972.
*Harris, James E., and Kent R. Weeks. *X-Raying the Pharaohs*. New York: Scribner's, 1973.
Herodotus. *Histories,* trans. A. de Selincourt. New York: Penguin Books, 1954.
Lucas, Alfred. *Ancient Egyptian Materials and Industries,* rev. J. R. Harris. New York: St. Martin's Press, 1962.
Maspero, Gaston. 'Les Momies Royales de Deir el-Baharî,' *Mémoires de la Mission Française Orientale du Caire,* Vol. I. Paris: 1889.
*Montet, Pierre. *Everyday Life in Egypt*. New York: Greenwood Press, 1974.
Winlock, Herbert E. *The Slain Soldiers of Nebhepetre Mentuhotpe*. New York: Macmillan, 1945.

CHAPTER THREE: Funerary Equipment

Winlock, Herbert E. *The Rise and Fall of the Middle Kingdom in Thebes*. New York: Macmillan, 1947.

CHAPTER FOUR: Funerals and Tombs

Funerals
Erman, Adolph. *Life in Ancient Egypt,* trans. H. M. Tirard. New York: Arno Press, Benjamin Blom, 1971.
Montet, Pierre. *Everyday Life in Egypt*. New York: Greenwood Press, 1974.

Tombs
Breasted, James H. *Ancient Records of Egypt*. New York: Russell & Russell, 1962.
Edwards, I. E. S. *The Pyramids of Egypt*. New York: Penguin Books, 1975.
Cerny, Jaroslav. *Ancient Egyptian Religion*. New York: Hillary House, 1957.

CHAPTER FIVE: Tomb Robberies

Harris, James E., and Kent R. Weeks. *X-Raying the Pharaohs*. New York: Scribner's, 1973.
Peet, T. E. *The Great Tomb Robberies*. London: Oxford University Press, 1940.
Simpson, W. Kelly. *The Literature of Ancient Egypt*. New Haven: Yale University Press, 1973.
Wilson, John A. *The Culture of Ancient Egypt*. Chicago: University of Chicago Press, 1956.

CHAPTER SIX: Amarna, Tutankhamun and Tanis

Aldred, Cyril. *Akhenaten, Pharaoh of Egypt*. New York: McGraw-Hill, 1971.
Carter, Howard. *The Tomb of Tutankhamen*. New York: Cooper Square Publishers, 1973.
Desroches-Noblecourt, C. *Tutankhamen*. New York: New York Graphic Society, 1976.

CHAPTER SEVEN: The Mummies and Europe

Harris, James E., and Kent R. Weeks. *X-Raying the Pharaohs*. New York: Scribner's, 1973.

GENERAL

Gardiner, Alan H. *Egypt of the Pharaohs*. New York: Oxford University Press, 1966.
Hayes, William C. *The Scepter of Egypt*. New York: New York Graphic Society, 1959. 2 vols.
Montet, Pierre. *Eternal Egypt*. New York: Praeger Publishers, 1970 (reissue).
Posener, Georges. *A Dictionary of Egyptian Civilization*. New York: Tudor Books, 1961.

It will be noticed that many of the books included in this bibliography were first published many years ago. The reason is that in the past half-century there have been no really major Egyptological discoveries which make these 'classics' any the less valuable, except in details and in style. There have indeed been great advances in scholarship since they were written—notably in the understanding of the Egyptian language—and much new evidence has been brought to light. But nothing has yet been found that radically alters the broad outlines of this ancient civilization as delineated by the scholars of Egyptology fifty years ago. Hence any new book for the general reader is bound to be, to some extent, a reworking of old and familiar material. The present authors acknowledge their debt to the 'classics' of

Egyptology, but have done their utmost to improve on their information where modern scholarship allows.

The books marked with an asterisk are those which have been of particular help to the authors, who would also like to mention the *British Museum General Introductory Guide to the Egyptian Collections* and a chapter in the *Cambridge Ancient History* by J. Cerny which deals with Egypt from the death of Ramesses III to the end of the 21st Dynasty.

ACKNOWLEDGEMENTS

The authors wish to thank the following for permission to reproduce illustrations in this book.

THE BRITISH MUSEUM for the illustrations on pages: 14, 18, 19, 22, 34, 40, 48, 50, 54 (right), 57, 59, 60, 70, 71, 77, 78, 80, 84, 86, 90, 92, 96, 129, 136, 139, 140, 145, 149, 175, 177, 181;

THE ASHMOLEAN MUSEUM Oxford for the illustration on page 165;

RADIO TIMES HULTON PICTURE LIBRARY for the illustrations on pages 171, 173;

BILDARCHIV PREUSSISCHER KULTURBESITZ for the illustration on page 164;

JOHN WEBB for the illustrations on pages 38, 52, 54 (left), 67, 69, 74, 82, 89, 194 and for the jacket photo.

The remaining illustrations are the copyright of CAROL ANDREWS.

They also wish to thank DR EDWARDS for permission to reproduce diagrams from his book *The Pyramids of Egypt*, Penguin Books;

Thanks are also due to Peter Smith who drew the tomb plans, Sue Hitches for the map, and Colin Reed for his assistance.

INDEX

Note: Page numbers in bold type refer to an illustration.

Ochre 51
Offering table **112**
Ogdoad 27, 29, 31
Old Kingdom 12, 16, 20, 24–5, 37, 112,
  114, 118, 124, 130, 136–7, 139, 143–4,
  146
Ombos 21
Onions 51
Opening of the Mouth 78, 101–2
Osiris 20–5, 28, 72, 75, 77, 78, 81, 83, 85,
  94, 125, 126, 127, 206
Osiris bed 72
Osorkon II 177
Ottoman Empire 189
Oxen 98, 101, 102

P

Paheri 130
Paikharu 148, 150–1, 152
Palace façade 108
Palette 34
Palm 99, 105
Panther skin 97, 102
Papyrus vignettes 100, 128
Paré, A. 182
Paser 148–153
Paweraa 148–153
Pectoral 76, 95, 178
Penhasi 175
Penicher, L. 189–90
Pepy II 203
Petrie, W. M. F. 139–40
Pharaoh 15–6, 64–5, 94, 105, 118, 155,
  166, 176
Pillar 112, 114, 119, 123, 124
Plug 137
Plutarch 21
Pole star 117
Porch 112, 120, 123
Portcullis 109, 137
Portrait panel 79
Pottery 33, 52, 93, 178
Pre-dynastic Period 28, 33
Pr-nfr 44
Psusennes 177
Ptah 27, 29, 62
Ptahhotep 130
Ptah-Sokaris-Osiris 77, 88
Ptolemaic Period 52, 53, 63, 91
Pyramid 61, 65, 113–9, 123, 124, 136,
  137, 141, 143, 146, 179
Pyramidion 114, 117, 119–20, 123

Pyramidology 205
Pyramid temple 117
Pyramid Texts 125–6

Q

Qebhsenuef 85, 91
Qurneh 153, 156

R

Ram 28, 77, 126, 127
Ramesses II 155, 184, 203
Ramesses III 58
Ramesses IV 49
Ramesses V 49
Ramesses VI 125
Ramesses IX 148
Ramesses XI 87
Ramesside Period 121, 128, 176
Ramose 128
Re 25–8, 29, 76–7, 84, 125–6, 146, 159,
  160
Re-Horakhty 78
Re-Horakhty-Atum 77
Rekhmire 16
Reserve head 68
Resin 36, 44, 47, 48, 49, 51
Rishi 75
Rock-cut tombs 111–2, 119–21, 123–4,
  146–7
Roman Period 52, 53, 63, 79
Rosetta Stone 184
Rostjau 126
Royal mummies 53, 55, 152, 155, 156,
  178
Ruaben 109

S

Saff tombs 119, 120, 124
Saite Period 70, 93
Sand graves 33, 34, 35, 107, 118
Saqqara 62, 107, 109, 179, 181, 190
Sarcophagus 66, 73, 94, 103, 177
Sawdust 49, 63
Scarab 66, 77, 85, 87
Scribe 95
Scribe *shabti* 69
Second Intermediate Period 68, 124,
  146, 158
Sekhemkhat 113
Sekhmet 14
Sem-priest 97, 99, 101, 102, 184